Uniforms of Marengo

Napoleonic Uniforms of the French Consular Army of Reserve and the Austrian Imperial Army of the Italian campaign in 1800

All Rights Reserved

No part of this book including images and artwork may be reproduced in any form by photocopying or by any electronic or mechanical means, including information storage or retrieval systems, without permission in writing from both the copyright owner and the publisher of this book

Copyright © DEAD DON'T TALK PUBLICATIONS 2023

ISBN 978-1-7396950-8-8 First Published 2023

Illustrator and author: EPM Gerard

Co-author: A Blanfurt

Publishing Editor and Illustrator: GP Musetti

DEAD DON'T TALK PUBLICATIONS
London
Email: infoDDTP@yahoo.com

Other Titles in the series:

- Uniforms of Austerlitz
- Uniforms of Jena
- Uniforms of Blenheim

When the division was formed in a semi-circle, the First Consul asked to address them: "The fields of Italy," he said, "will be, for you, a storehouse of plenty. I've already told some of you this, four years ago. In these fields, an arrogant enemy awaits us. You are, just like your predecessors who followed me at Lodi and Montenotte, badly dressed, badly fed and still unpaid.
In fifteen days, all this will be changed. Soldiers, I will ask of you one great effort before you meet with the Austrians. Follow me with confidence and you will return covered in glory, having saved our country, which is once again threatened by foreigners."
Letter of General Boudet to Dubreton, quoting Bonaparte

The true events of Marengo bring honour to the Austrian army, even if Providence allowed us ultimately to succumb. Those who fought at Marengo carry the knowledge that they fulfilled their duty to Monarch and Fatherland with loyalty and courage. I call on all Frenchmen who were at Marengo to tell me if I speak the truth. Yes, I call on Napoleon himself as my witness. In these past ten years, others have deigned to lecture us on what we could have done better or what strategies we should have taken; I acknowledge their advice. Yet if you want to learn lessons for the future, it might be better to look at the true course of events, setting them out in detail over the time and space that constitute reality.
Joseph von Stutterheim – Report on the Battle of Marengo.

With Napoleon, passion and power united themselves with a thirst for glory; each served to stimulate the other and activate an ardent energy: he wanted to achieve glory through power and power through a glory, the like of which mortal men have never achieved and will never achieve on earth; but as his genius was commensurate to his vast ambition, he believed he was certain to achieve it.
Victor: Extraits des Mémoires inédits

My Lord, you are preparing to fight against men who dress in rough raw-hide. So harsh is their life that they eat as much as they have, never as much as they want. They drink no wine, but only water. They have no goods at all. If you attack them, what can you possibly gain? But once they experience your wealth and luxury, they will hold on so tightly that nothing will make them let go.
Advice of Sandanis the Lydian to King Croesus: Herodotus

Contents

1. Order of Battle — Page 5
2. Maps and Photographs — Page 10
3. The Campaign and Battle — Page 20
4. The Austrian Army in 1800 — Page 37
5. The French Army in 1800 — Page 104
6. Index of artists and Bibliography — Page 207

Order of Battle
(With references to Maps below)

Numbers and positions of troops are, at best, general estimates based on available sources. Any order of battle for this era must by its very nature be an approximation.

Even where precise figures for a regiment exist, this is no indication of the number of men fielded on the day of the battle, which would tend to be lower. The figures for the French are taken from Cugnac and based on War Ministry returns published in 1803. The figures for the Austrians are based on written sources drawn up prior to the battle by the High Command. Finally, the order of battle is arranged according to who actually commanded each unit during the battle itself.

The French Army of Reserve at Marengo
Total estimated strength – 28,170 men
Cavalry – 3,740:   Artillery – 690:   Infantry – 23,740:

First Consul: Napoleon Bonaparte   Commander in Chief: Louis Alexandre Berthier
Commanding Cavalry: Lt Gen Joachim Murat   Commanding Artillery: Gen Marmont

1. Defending Marengo: Total: 11,280 men
Under the command of Lieutenant General Victor
These figures include the men and units defending the front line at Marengo from early morning on 14th June.

Gardanne's Division
- 44th Ligne   3 Btn   1,750 men
- 101st Ligne   3 Btn   1,890

(Olivier) Rivaud's Division (Chambarlhac)
- 43rd Ligne   3 Btn   1,900 men
- 96th Ligne   3 Btn   1,590
- 24th Legere   3 Btn   1,800

Kellermann's Heavy Brigade
- 2nd Cavalerie   3 Sqn   120 men
- 20th Cavalerie   3 Sqn   350
- 21st Cavalerie   1 Plt   50

Champeaux's Dragoon Brigade
- 1st Dragoons   4 Sqn   450
- 8th Dragoons   4 Sqn   330
- 9th Dragoons   3 Sqn   220

Duvignau's Light Cavalry Brigade
(Duvignau had been injured the night before the battle in a riding accident and was not at the battle).
- 6th Dragoons   4 Sqn   300
- 12th Chasseurs   (detached – see below)
- 11th Hussars   2 Sqn   200

- 4th Company 5th Horse Artillery	4 guns	100
- 10th Company 6th Horse Artillery	3 guns	100
- Artillery Train		130

2. Reinforcing northern flank of Marengo: Total: 5,190 men
Under the command of Lieutenant General Lannes
These troops arrived during the course of the early afternoon.

Watrin's Division
- 28th Ligne	3 Btn	1,000 men
- 22nd Ligne	3 Btn	1,260
- 40th Ligne	3 Btn	1,720
- 6th Legere	3 Btn	1,110
- 2nd Company 2nd Horse Artillery	4 guns	100

3. Counter-attacking on northern flank of Battlefield: Total: 4,930 men
Under the command of the First Consul, Napoleon Bonaparte
These troops arrived during mid-afternoon, just as the French retreat commenced

Monnier's Division
- 70th Ligne	3 Btn	1,460 men
- 72nd Ligne	3 Btn	1,240
- 19th Legere	2 Btn	910
- 5th Company 1st Artillery Reg*	4 guns	60

Consular Guard Infantry
- Grenadiers and Chasseurs a pied	1 Btn	800 men

Consular Guard Cavalry
- Grenadiers a Cheval	1 Sqn	240 men
- Chasseurs a Cheval	1 Sqn	120 men
- Guard Horse Artillery	6 guns	100

4. Counter-attacking at Cascina Grossa: Total: 5,710 men
Under the command of Lieutenant General Desaix
These troops arrived on the battlefield at about 5 o'clock and deployed for action shortly before 6 o'clock

Boudet's Division
- 30th Ligne	3 Btn	1,430 men
- 59th Ligne	3 Btn	1,870
- 9th Legere	3 Btn	2,010
- 4th Company 2nd Horse Artillery	8 guns	100

Desaix's cavalry
- 3rd Cavalerie	2 Sqn	150 men

Order of Battle

- 1st Hussars　　　　　　　　　　　　　1 Sqn　　　　　　　　150 men

5. Detached to far northern and southern flanks of battlefield: Total: 1,060 men
These troops participated in the battle indirectly and at the very end of the battle
(Jean) Rivaud's Brigade
- 21st Chasseurs　　　　　　　　　　　4 Sqn　　　　　　　　360 men
- 12th Hussars　　　　　　　　　　　　4 Sqn　　　　　　　　400
Detached from Duvignau's Brigade
- 12th Chasseurs　　　　　　　　　　　4 Sqn　　　　　　　　300

*The artillery park at Torre Garofoli would have included artillerymen from various companies. All these would have been ordered to Marengo, so it is possible that detachments from other artillery units were present at the battle. Furthermore, a further 5 guns arrived from the park in time to be used by Desaix.

The Austrian Army of Italy at Marengo
Total estimated strength – 31,880 men
Cavalry – 7,550:　　Cavalry Artillery – 800:　　Infantry – 23,530:
Commander in Chief: GdK Michael von Melas. Chief of Staff: GM Anton von Zach

1. First Main Column: Attacking Marengo　　　　Total: 18,240 men
Under the command of General Melas and General-Major Zach

Advance Guard　　　　　　　　　　　　　　　　　　　1,150 men
- 3rd Bach Light Inf. Battalion　　　　　(detached to Second Column)
- 4th Am Ende Light Inf. Battalion　　　1 Btn　　　　　　　290
- Mariassy Jager Companies　　　　　　5 Cmp　　　　　　200
- Pioneer Company　　　　　　　　　　1 Cmp　　　　　　100
- Bussy Horse Jager　　　　　　　　　　2 Sqn　　　　　　　190
- 1st Kaiser Dragoons　　　　　　　　　2 Sqn　　　　　　　270
- Cavalry Artillery Battery　　　　　　　6 guns　　　　　　100

Fieldmarshal-Lieutenant Hadik's Brigade　　　　　　　5,320 men
- 52nd Erzherzog Anton Hungarian Reg.　2 Btn　　　　　　860
- 53rd Jellacic Hungarian Reg.　　　　　2 Btn　　　　　　610
- 11th Michael Wallis Reg.　　　　　　　3 Btn　　　　　　2,210
- 47th Franz Kinsky Reg.　　　　　　　　3 Btn　　　　　　1,640

(14 battalion guns)

Fieldmarshal-Lieutenant Kaim's Brigade　　　　　　　3,300 men
- 23rd Grossherzog von Toscana Reg.　　3 Btn　　　　　　2,190

- 63rd Erzherzog Joseph Reg.   3 Btn   1,110
(14 battalion guns)

General-Major Lattermann's Grenadier Brigade — **2,220 men**
- Parr Battalion   1 Btn   360
- St Julien Battalion   1 Btn   380
- Schiaffinati Battalion   1 Btn   410
- Kleinmayer Battalion   1 Btn   380
- Weber Battalion   1 Btn   390
- Pioneers   2 Cpm   300

(10 battalion guns)

General-Major Weidenfeld's Grenadier Brigade — **2,520 men**
- Khevenholler Battalion   1 Btn   380
- Pieret Battalion   1 Btn   230
- Pertusi Battalion   1 Btn   560
- Perss Battalion   1 Btn   290
- Gorschen Battalion   1 Btn   290
- Weissenwolf Battalion   1 Btn   490
- Pioneers   2 Cpm   280

(12 battalion guns)

General Pilatti's Dragoon Brigade — **1,360 men**
- 1st Kaiser Dragoons   3 Sqn   310 men
- 4th Karaczay Dragoons   6 Sqn   1,050

General Nobili's Dragoon Brigade — **1,870 men**
- 3rd Erzherzog Johann Dragoons   6 Sqn   860
- 9th Lichtenstein Dragoons   6 Sqn   1,010

Reserve Artillery
- 5 Cavalry Artillery Batteries   30 guns   500 men

2. Second Column: Northern Flank of Battlefield   Total: **8,240 men**
Under the command of Fieldmarshal-Lieutenant Ott

General-Major Gottesheim's Advance Guard — **1,290 men**
- 3rd Bach Light Inf. Battalion   1 Btn   280
- Mariassy Jager Companies   1 Cmp   40
- Pioneer Company   1 Cmp   100
- 28th Frohlich Lieb Battalion   1 Btn   520

Order of Battle

- 10th Lobkowitz Dragoons	2 Sqn	250
- Cavalry Artillery Battery	6 guns	100

Fieldmarshal-Lieutenant Schellenberg's Brigade — **4,510 men**
- 51st Splenyi Hungarian Reg.	2 Btn	740
- 57th Colloredo Reg.	3 Btn	1,370
- 28th Frohlich Reg.	2 Btn	1,050
- 40th Mittrowsky Reg.	3 Btn	850
- 10th Lobkowitz Dragoons	4 Sqn	500

(14 battalion guns; two 6-pounders and two 12-pounders)

Fieldmarshal-Lieutenant Vogelsang's Brigade — **2,190 men**
- 18th Stuart Reg.	3 Btn	1,280
- 17th Hohenlohe Reg.	2 Btn	910

(7 battalion guns)

Major Krapf's Engineer Companies — **250 men**
- Pontoneer Company.	1 Cmp	60
- Sapper Company.	1 Cmp	90
- Miner Company.	1 Cmp	100

3. Third Column: Southern Flank of Battlefield — Total: 3,060 men
Under the command of Fieldmarshal-Lieutenant O'Reilly

Grenzer Infantry — **2,290 men**
- 3rd Oguliner Grenz Regiment	1 Btn	600
- 5th Warasdin-Kreuz Grenz Regiment	1 Btn	760
- 2nd Ottocac Grenz Regiment	1 Btn	300
- 4th Banat District Grenz Battalion	1 Btn	530
- Cavalry Artillery Battery	6 guns	100

Third Column Hussar Brigade — **770 men**
- 8th Nauendorf Hussars	3 Sqn	430
- 5th Hussars	2 Sqn	230
- 8th Wurtemberg Light Dragoons	1 Sqn	110

4. General Numbsch's Hussar Brigade — Total: 2,340 men
Detached from First Column to protect southern approach to Alessandria
- 9th Erdody Hussars	6 Sqn	990
- 7th Hussars	8 Sqn	1,350

Maps and Photographs

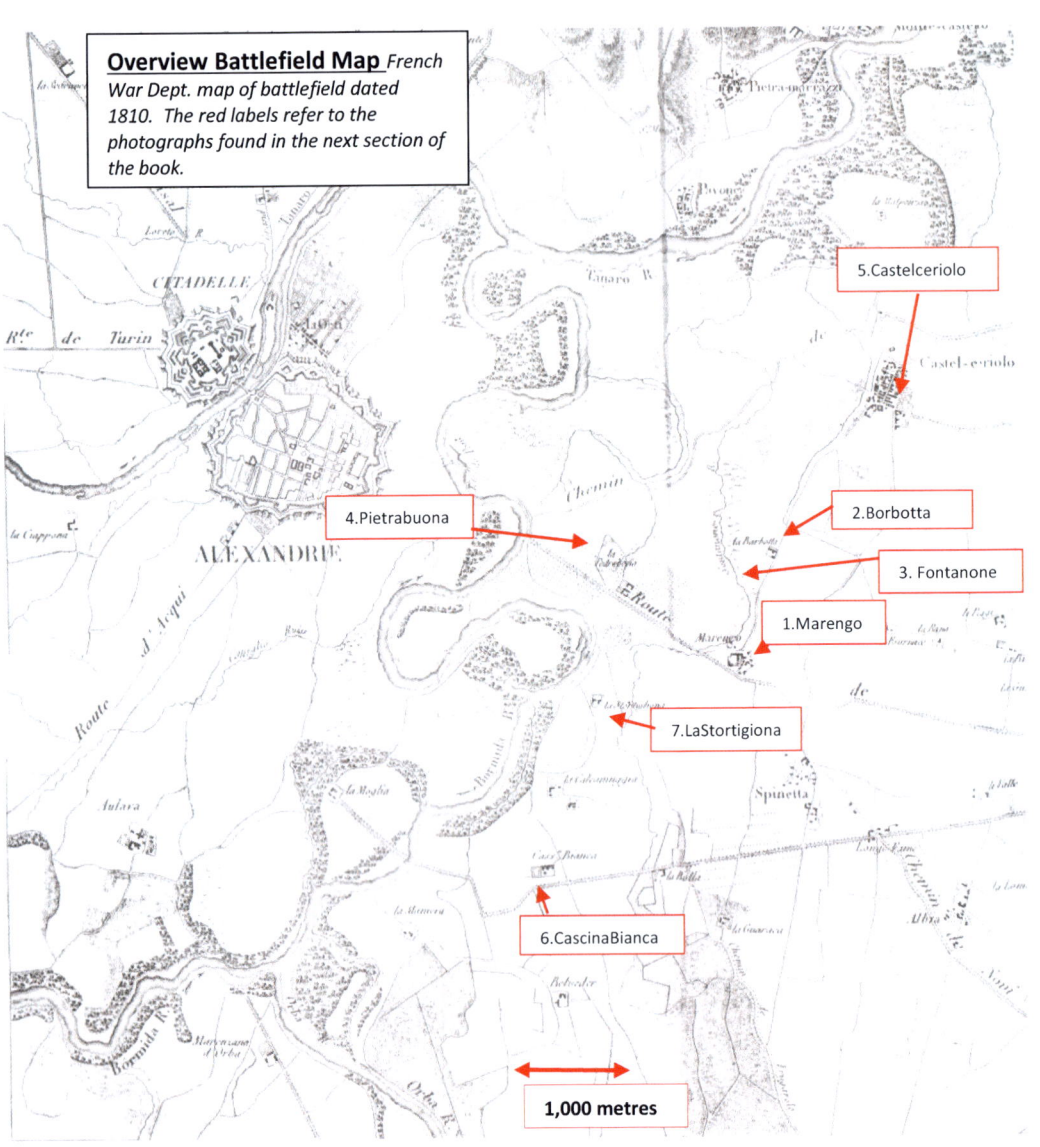

Maps and Photographs

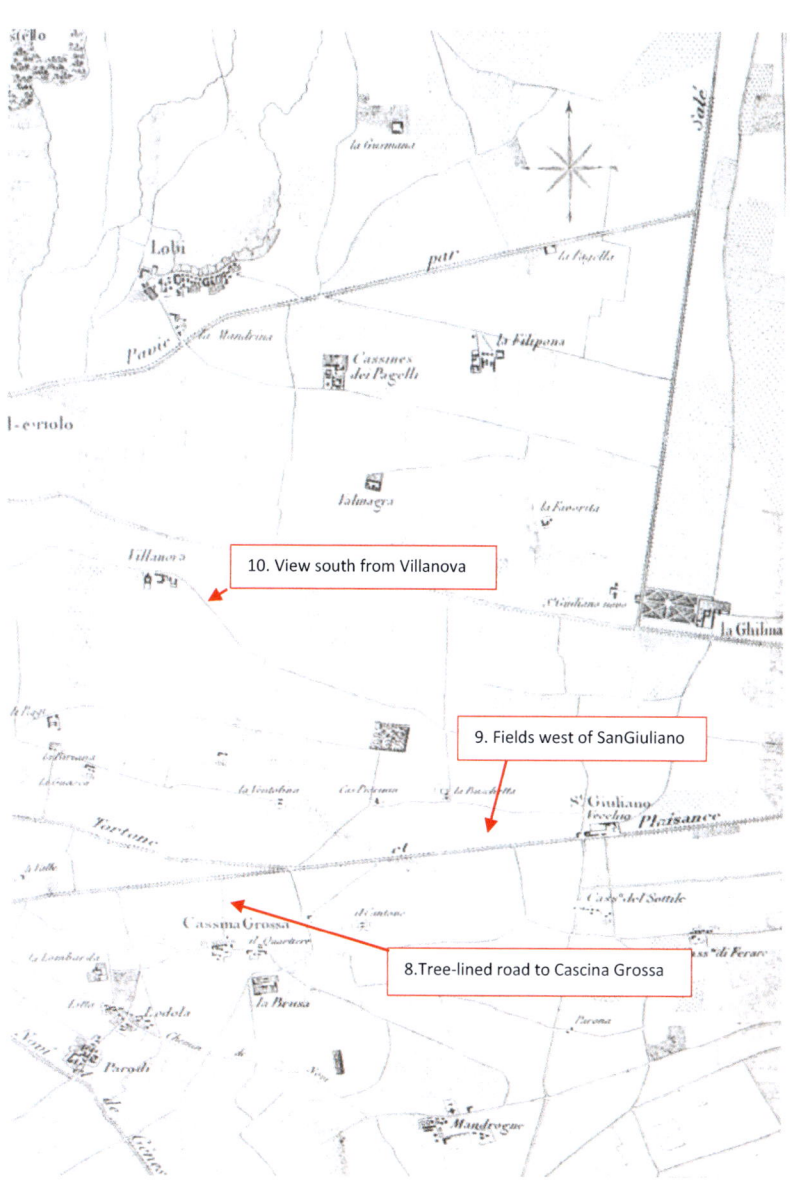

12   Maps and Photographs

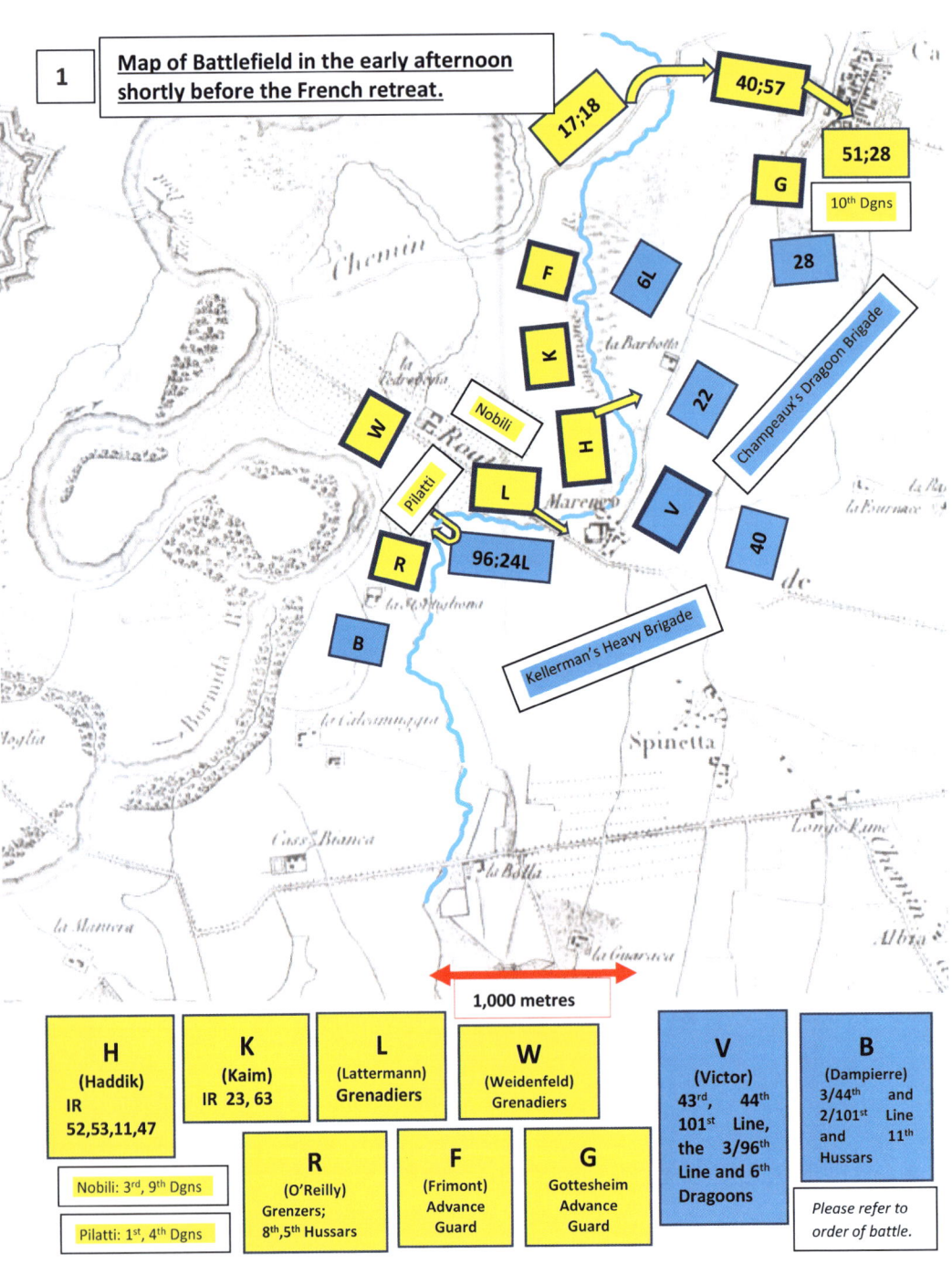

Maps and Photographs

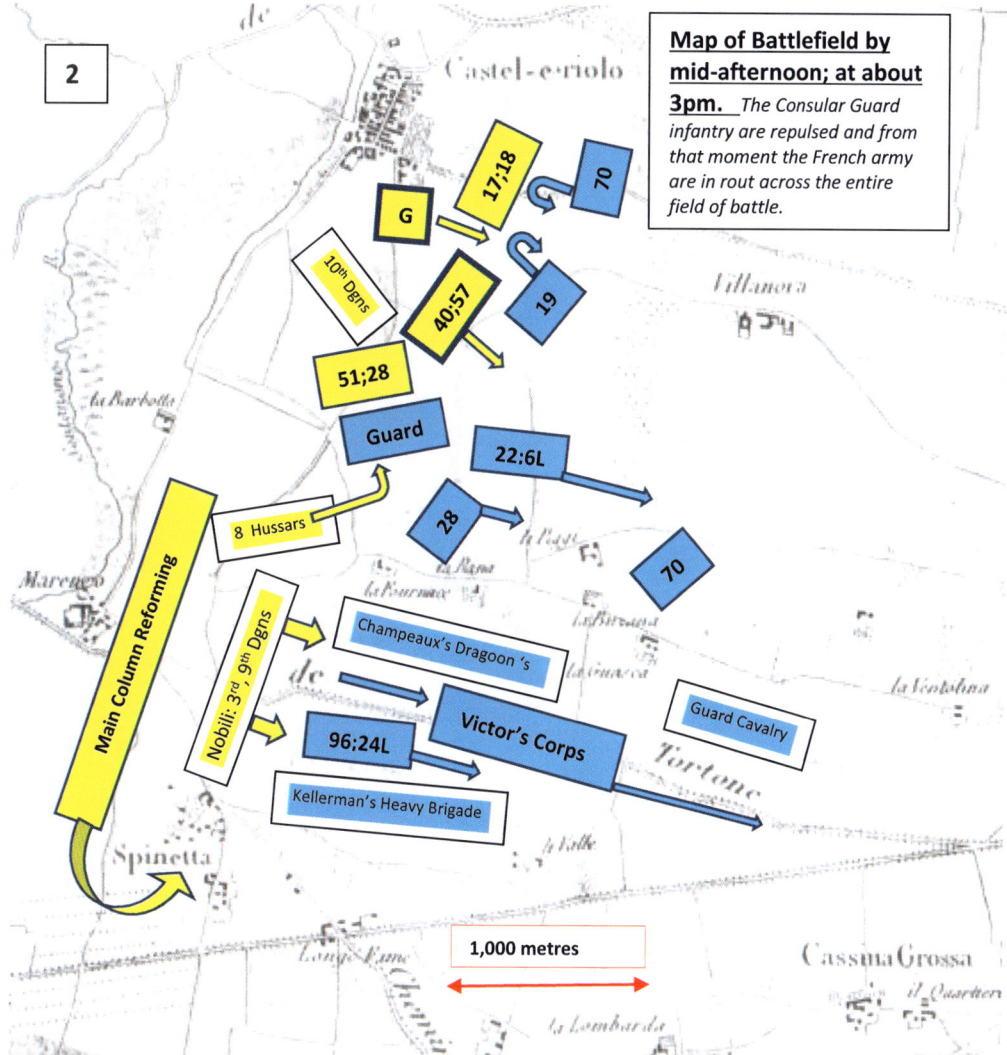

Maps and Photographs

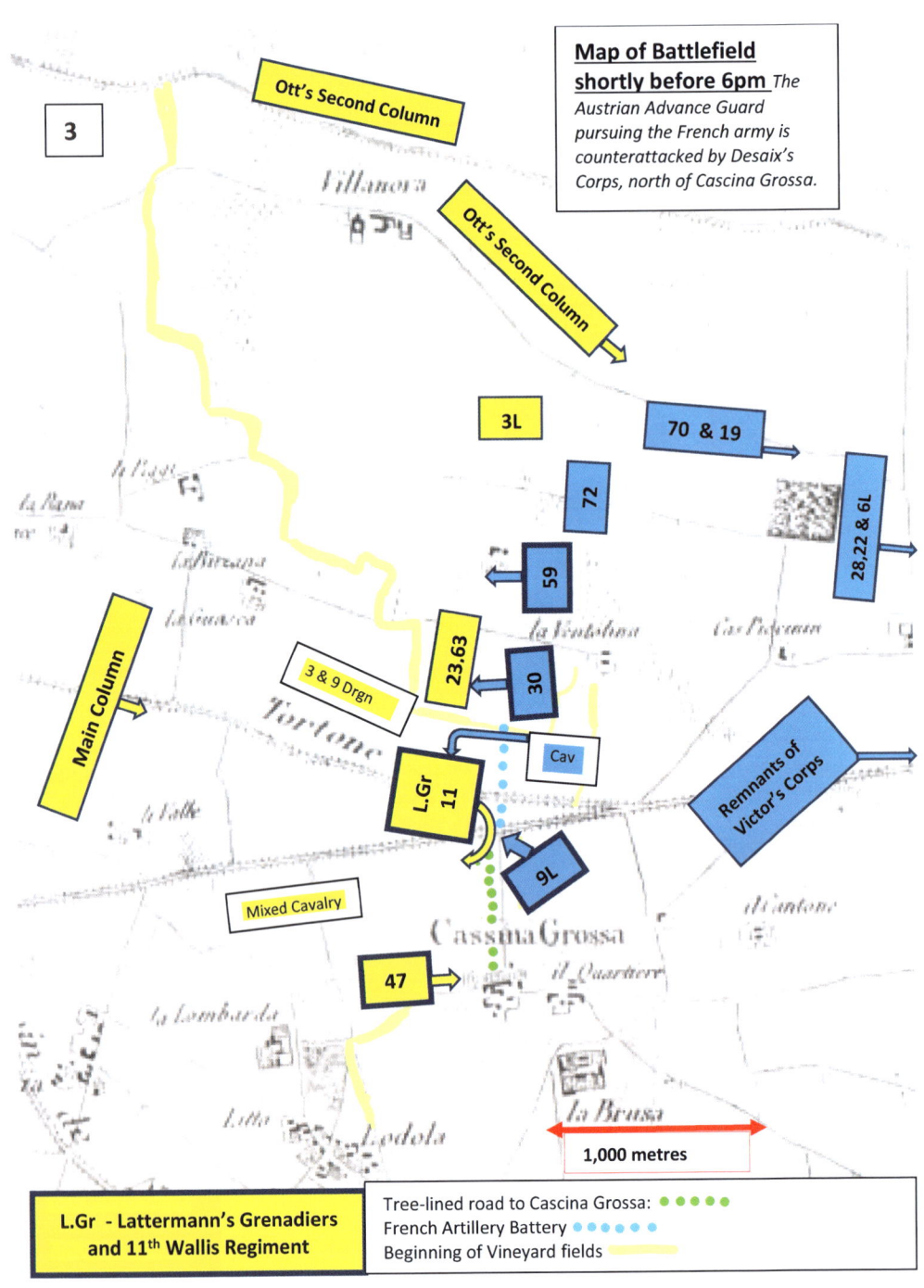

Maps and Photographs

1. MARENGO: The courtyard of Marengo. The early medieval tower and its circuit of brick farm buildings and walls. Still mostly unchanged.

1. MARENGO: The 100-200 metres between the Fontanone ditch on the right and the circuit of buildings at Marengo farm. The Fontanone today runs between high concrete banks.

2. THE FONTANONE DITCH: As it was then. Steep banked, marshy with thick vegetation. A three-metre wide ditch of stagnant water.

Maps and Photographs

8. THE SITE OF DESAIX'S COUNTER-ATTACK: As it appears today and as it appeared in the battle, with the spire of Cascina Grossa's church in the background and the tree-lined road to the left. Lejeune's painting (below) is a masterpiece of observation.

8. THE VIA DELLA LIBERTA: With its raised banks and trees, it provided a perfect site for a large-scale ambush.

Maps and Photographs

3. BORBOTTA FARM: Austrian grenadiers launched their first attacks on Marengo across this ground, from Borbotta in the distance. (Left of centre)

4. PIETRABUONA FARM: (Pederbona) These are the last few original remaining buildings.

5. CASTEL CERIOLO: The old town square behind the fortified manor house

5. CASTEL CERIOLO: Approached from the south along the Borbotta road.

6. CASCINA BIANCA: Or 'La Caleamuggia'- Both buildings lined Dampierre's retreat.

7. LA STORTIGLIONA FARM: With its raised tracks and ditches, it provided Dampierre's men with a first line of defence, before they became cut off.   It remains unchanged.

9. THE PLAIN: Between Marengo and San Giuliano – flat as a pancake.

10. VILLANOVA ROAD: Ott's Second Column advanced along this road, through fields still covered in orchards today.

10. VILLANOVA FARM : One of the many farms in the plain, all based around a central courtyard.

The Campaign

The Italian Campaign of 1800, opened with Bonaparte having established direct rule as first Consul in France through a coup d'etat. On 18th Brumaire (9th November 1799), he seized power through a military coup with the active support of a circle of close supporters and the acquiescence of key generals including General Jean Victor Moreau, the commander in Chief of the Army of the Rhine. His position at this stage was tenuous. The army and political atmosphere of 1799-1800 was still markedly republican. Bonaparte was surrounded by potential rivals and enemies who expected his rule to be as fleeting as those of his republican predecessors. What popular support he had, was based on his charisma and reputation as a successful military leader as well as his promise of a return to peace and stability. He needed to deliver on these expectations. Victory, peace and stable government.

Britain and Austria were equally determined to press their gains and their partial victories won in 1799. Austria in particular, through its foreign minister Johann Thugut, sought to reaffirm its control of Italy and southern Germany.

The focus of both France and Austria lay in Italy and both sides were preparing for a resumption of conflict in Spring 1800. In particular, the Austrian High Command in Italy predicted (correctly) that the French would begin a fresh campaign in late April 1800. The snows on the Alpine passes always melted in April and this meant that French armies could travel with their heavy supply and artillery trains – their life-blood. General Zach, the Austrian Chief of staff, calculated that the Austrians would have 6 weeks of good spring weather in March to mid-April before Bonaparte could return to Italy with a new army. Within this narrow window of time, he planned to defeat the remnants of the beleaguered French 'Army of Italy'. He could then concentrate on guarding the Alpine passes and prevent a new invasion.

Defeating the Army of Italy appeared an easy enough task. What little was left of it was starved of supplies, entrenched and isolated in fortified coastal towns along the Italian Apennines. Yet the Austrian campaign opened badly, with an abortive attack on Savona on 13th February, thwarted by political wrangling in the Austrian High Command. Officers were upset that the early date would clash with a society ball to be held in Turin; war would have to wait. When hostilities did reopen, the Austrian army was able to quickly divide the French in two, pushing forces under generals Suchet and Soult back towards Nice and trapping a second force under General Massena within the fortifications of the key port of Genoa. The siege of Genoa dragged on for two months, during which time an estimated 20-30,000 inhabitants died from the combined effects of starvation and typhus. With no news getting through, Massena eventually surrendered the city on the 4th June, thereby freeing up some 20,000 besieging Austrian troops. However, in focusing on the Army of Italy, the Austrians had failed to prevent Bonaparte from entering the campaign with a new army – the Army of Reserve.

Although aware that Bonaparte could enter Northern Italy through the Alpine passes, the Austrian High Command expected this to be a secondary route of invasion. The main French route into Italy was expected to be Nice with the French moving along the coastal Alps. Only the coastal route had roads wide enough for the heavy vehicles needed to supply an army with ammunition and artillery, let alone other provisions.

Bonaparte thought differently. Over the winter of 1799-1800, in a campaign of secrecy and misinformation, he had organized and equipped a new 'Army of Reserve' in France and along the borders with Switzerland. Even the name given to this force was misleading. In fact, it would include some of the best regiments France had to offer, newly equipped. Over the 14th-16th May, the first elements of this Army crossed the Alps. It was an army that included some 55,000 men, grouped in 5 major Corps. Moreover, they had entered Italy some 200 miles to the rear of the main Austrian army fighting along the coast. In the following two weeks, Bonaparte's divisions spread out over the Northern Italian plain, capturing key cities and road-networks. Milan on 2nd June and Piacenza on the 7th June with its bridge crossing the Po river. In doing so, he had effectively cut off the Austrian Army from its lines of communications and its territories in North-Eastern Italy. However, Bonaparte had only been able to cross with light Horse-Artillery and the Army of Reserve was increasingly short of ammunition and provisions. More importantly, the Austrian High Command was acutely aware of this weakness and planned to use it to their advantage.*

It is in this situation that the Austrian High Command headed by its ailing 74 year old Commander in Chief, General von Melas, and its more able Chief of Staff General Anton Zach, decided to concentrate their forces to meet this new threat. This concentration was to converge on the fortified city of Alessandria, replete with provisions and road networks. It is here that the Austrian High Command would decide how to react.

They were faced with two choices. The first was to avoid battle and reopen a passage across the Po river, re-establishing their lines of communications. The second option was to face Bonaparte's army and use their overwhelming superiority in cavalry and artillery to defeat him in open battle, thus simultaneously re-establishing their supply and communications. However, the Austrians would only risk a battle if it could be fought on favourable ground; ground on which their artillery and cavalry could operate.

There were few such areas in the hilly country that lay between the Austrians and French. However, to the east of Alessandria, was a plain that stretched 24 km from Alessandria's Bormida river to the Scrivia river near Tortona. This area and its road network was so strategically important that two smaller battles had already been fought there in 1799. Zach and Melas were in agreement that if Bonaparte could be drawn in to this area, the Austrian army would be able to face it in a position of superiority.

As the forward divisions of the French army under Lannes and Victor advanced, they fought an important engagement with the Austrians between the villages of Casteggio and Montebello on the 9th June. By the 13th June, the Austrians had withdrawn to the plain of Marengo, leaving a garrison at the town of Tortona on the eastern edge of the plain and a forward position at Marengo. The Austrian plan was to gather their forces at Alessandria and then attack the French in the plain. In doing this, Zach took great pains to mislead Bonaparte, feeding him misinformation about plans to retreat and bridge the Po at Casale to the north-east. Zach even detached his Pontoneer corps to construct a pontoon bridge there.

At this point, the Austrians committed a serious mistake. Their forward positions were left guarded by perhaps the weakest unit of their army. Commanded by FML O'Reilly, this was made up of 4 battalions of 'Grenzer' irregular troops. When attacked by the French on the evening of 13th June, they abandoned Marengo, retreating behind the heavily defended bridgehead crossing the Bormida river at Alessandria.

In doing this, the Austrians had allowed the French to occupy ground that would deny them access to the plain beyond. In reality this was due to gross incompetence on the part of the Austrian High Command. However, Bonaparte saw it as final proof that the Austrians would not seek a battle and were intent on merely escaping across the Po. He made his dispositions accordingly, leaving the five available divisions of his army strung along a 15km route from the Bormida to the Scrivia, and sending General Desaix' Corps to reconnoitre another 15km to the south. Despite the loss of Marengo, the Austrian High Command proceeded with their plan and over the night of 13th-14th June prepared their army on the western bank of the Bormida.

(*In crossing the Alps, French bulletins placed their focus on the problems encountered in bypassing the Austrian stronghold at fort Bard. Whilst the siege of Fort Bard presented a very real obstacle, *correspondence between Napoleon and his High Command show that he had seriously under-estimated the problems in bringing artillery through the passes, let alone in keeping it supplied. As in all things, he appears to have made a high stakes gamble; hoping to capture Austrian ordnance en route.)*

The Battlefield and Opposing Forces

"The night was so pure and still that an attentive ear could listen to even the slightest sound that might break the calm. Then at about one o'clock in the morning, whilst all was quiet on the plain, one began to hear, from the far bank of the Bormida, a noise, muffled but intense, as of a multitude moving and gathering.

Then the rolling beat of drums and the blasts of bugles, together with the sound of horses and the more strident rumble of wagons and cannon on the move. One could no longer doubt that the enemy were preparing for battle and so we waited anxiously for the day. Dawn slowly began to lighten the horizon and soon one of the most radiant Italian suns illuminated the scene. Before us, we could see the entire Austrian army under arms. To the eye, I judged it to be 25,000 infantry, 6-7,000 cavalry and a formidable artillery." Victor.

The General Staffs of both armies knew this battlefield very well. Many of the officers and men waking that morning had been there before, in 1799 or in previous campaigns. To understand the sequences of events that were to unfold that day, one must understand the importance and nature of the battlefield itself. The road network between Alexandria and Tortona formed a key passage between the Apennine mountains to the south and the rich agricultural plains and cities of the northern plain. From here one could take routes to Genoa, Milan or Turin. It also formed the border between the French and Austrian controlled territories. In planning the campaign, Bonaparte fully expected the Austrians to fight here and for their part, the Austrians did everything they could to lure the French on to this battleground. They had good reasons for this.

Skirting the edge of the Apennines, the region afforded one of the first areas of plain in which cavalry and artillery could operate to full advantage. In 1800, the plain was given over to intensive agriculture including wheat, corn and vines. It was irrigated and drained by a series of ditches which cut through fields and also ran alongside most of the roads. Running north to south, in front of Marengo was the irrigation canal 'Fontanone' which was to play such a key feature in the battle. Although now diminished and banked in concrete, at the time, it measured 2-3 metres across with steep marshy banks on either side. It served as a flood barrier and as an overflow channel for the Bormida, to which it was connected. Deep, stagnant, steep banked and boggy, the Fontanone was brim-full with river water from the recent heavy rainfall.

The wide area of cultivated fields and good road networks were to the east of the Fontanone – an area which was already held by the French on the morning of the battle. The ground to the west of the Fontanone up to the river was boggy and wooded, being a natural flood-plain; it is to this area that the Austrians were now confined. Along this north-south line of the Fontanone were a series of large farm complexes. Based around courtyards with a perimeter of walls, gatehouses and barns, they included the farms of La Stortigliona and Cascina Bianca to the south and La Barbotta to the north and Pietrabuona (Pedrabona) and Marengo itself along the line of the central Alessandria-Tortona road. Marking the far northern point of this line was the village of Castel-Ceriolo based around its fortified manor house. It is along this line that the majority of the battle unfolded during the course of the day, with the Austrians trying to force their way into the open plain on the other side of the Fontanone. (See Map 1 above)

Running through this plain, east to west was the Alessandria – Tortona road along which the main Austrian force planned to advance. It was marked by the Pietrabuona (Pederbona) farm, the Marengo farm and hamlet and by the village of Cascina Grossa and village of San Giuliano, marking the centre and eastern extent of the battlefield. Both villages were dominated by the bell-towers of their churches. Although very flat, visibility and movement at ground-level was severely restricted by crops, trees and vineyards, criss-crossed by drainage ditches. *"In the plains of Italy, one cannot see very far. Every field is surrounded by rows of trees on which grow vines tied from one tree to the other, hanging like garlands. Many fields are walled or enclosed with deep, wide ditches."* Stutterheim.

In the early hours of the morning the French outposts at Marengo could clearly hear the sound of an army in motion. As dawn broke, from the high tower of Marengo, General Victor was able to observe the Austrian army filing out of their fortified bridgehead on the Bormida. From 5am-9am he watched the different divisions and artillery trains take up positions. Urgent messages were being sent to Bonaparte at Torre Garofoli, over 10 km away on the eastern edge of the plain.

Bonaparte had simply not expected the Austrians to fight. As a consequence, only two demi-brigades held the front line, the 101st and the 44th Ligne. During the course of the morning, Generals Victor, Lannes and Watrin were able to bring up a further 7 infantry demi-brigades to defend the line of the Fontanone; a total of over 9,000 infantry, backed by the 2,000 cavalry of the Dragoon and Heavy Cavalry brigades.

Bonaparte was frantically recalling all the reinforcements he could muster – these would begin to arrive on the battlefield during the course of the afternoon. Close at hand, he could count on the Consular Guard and three infantry demi-brigades (the 70th and 72nd Ligne and 19th Legere), a reinforcement of about 4,500 foot and 360 horse. Further afield, some 15 kilometres away, he sent increasingly desperate messages to recall a further three demi-brigades commanded by Lieutenant-General Desaix, a final reinforcement of 5,700 men which he hoped would arrive by the close of day.

On the morning of the 14th June, these troops found themselves at the end of a very tenuous supply chain stretching back over the Alps. They lacked artillery, having about 35 guns. There were few reserve cartridges and even less ammunition and powder for the cannons. In his anxiety to force a battle on the Austrians, Bonaparte had placed his army in an extremely vulnerable position. If the Austrians pushed the fighting into the open plain, he would not have the men, cavalry or the artillery to stand up to them. It was vital to stop them at the Fontanone.

Facing the French, in full battle array, with flags and regimental bands was the Austrian Imperial Army of Italy. The Austrian Army had been fundamentally weakened by two arduous years of campaigning in Italy throughout 1799 and 1800. Yet Generals Melas and Zach had collected the very best units of their army for the battle – these included eleven Grenadier battalions and their elite cavalry and light artillery units. Totalling 23,500 infantry and artillery and 7,500 cavalry with over 80 guns, they were well provisioned and in very good morale.

The Austrian plan called for an attack in three columns. The main column of over 14,500 infantry and 6,000 cavalry would push their way through Marengo and along the open plain to San Giuliano.

A 'Second Column' of about 7,500 foot and 750 cavalry would advance north towards Castel Ceriolo and then to Sale.

They would be flanked to the South by the weakest element of the army, some 2,300 Grenzer infantry, strengthened by about 800 Hungarian Hussars of the 8th and 5th regiments, led by FML O'Reilly.

These three columns would gain control of the plain and re-establish their line of communications with Austria and the hereditary lands, defeating the French in the process.

The Austrians heavily outnumbered the French in cavalry and artillery and it was in these weapons that they placed their confidence. However, in infantry they were attacking a force which was roughly equivalent to their own, even without Desaix's three regiments. Moreover, they would be attacking this large body of infantry on initially unfavourable ground, where their superiority in cavalry and artillery could not be used.

The Battle

"At any moment we expected this great army to advance. But as the minutes turned to hours, it remained motionless. Some claimed that the loss of Marengo had delayed the assault...whatever the reason, more than four hours passed before they were ordered to attack.
In this interval, their troops were given rations and brandy in good measure. We later learnt that they had also been given new supplies, new clothing and 5 days pay in advance. Our own troops matched them in courage and morale, even though they were poorly fed, badly dressed and seldom paid. Then at 8 o'clock, these masses, hitherto motionless, began to advance." Victor

During the four hour wait, Melas and Zach saw fit to detach over 2000 hussars to recross the Bormida and reconnoitre to the south of Alessandria; thereby weakening their army. The battle opened at 9am with light infantry Jagers and Grenzers of the Austrian Advance Guard attacking the French forward positions held by the 101st and 44th Demi-Brigades. This forward position ran either side of the road flanked by two strong farm complexes. PietraBuona farm, some 250 metres to the north and La Stortigliona 700 metres to the south-east.
Commanding the 101st and 44th was the 42 year old General Gaspard Gardanne and the overall commander of this advance Corps was the even younger 36 year old Claude Victor Perrin – known as General Victor. Victor ordered Gardanne and his men to take the brunt of the initial attack and bombardment, before falling back to the more defensible line of the Fontanone canal. The fighting along this initial front line lasted well over an hour, with the two Demi-Brigades withdrawing methodically from PietraBuona but continuing to hold La Stortigliona.

Moving past Pietrabuona, Victor's account describes how the Austrians fanned out on either side of the road, reforming their front line with artillery at the front. Their Third Column veered south and a final 'Second' Column began to move north. The main Austrian Column was drawn up in three large battle-columns stacked one behind the other along the road, with the fusilier regiments to the front and the elite Grenadier battalions kept in reserve.

From 10.30am to 1pm the Austrian main column attempted successive attacks along the Old Tortona Road and to either side of it, in an effort to cross the Fontanone and capture the central French position at Marengo. The first attack was made by General Bellegarde's 52nd and 53rd Hungarian Infantry regiments supported by the 11th and 47th Infantry. The Hungarian regiments were considered the best in the army and by any estimation, this attack should have succeeded in opening a way beyond Marengo.   However, the Austrians had seriously under-estimated the firepower of the French troops lining the Fontanone.

Over the course of the following 2-3 hours the French fed more and more reinforcements into the battle. By 12 noon General Victor had replaced what remained of the 101st and 44th with his three remaining demi-brigades; the 43rd and 96th Ligne and 24th Legere. Over the following hour, four other demi-brigades belonging to General Lanne's Corps would also arrive. These included the 28th, 22nd and 40th demi-brigades as well as the 6th Legere. By about 1pm, these had taken up flanking positions to the north of Marengo, as far as Castel Ceriolo.

The fighting had degenerated into a battle of attrition with infantry and artillery firing at each other a very short range across the canal which now divided the armies. Along this meandering line of the Fontanone, soldiers were being deployed in small units along the banks, often fighting as light infantry. Coignet, even though a grenadier, was employed in this way:

'I found myself running behind the trunk of a tall willow tree, from where I continued to fire as best I could. However, the fire was so heavy that I soon had to throw myself to the ground, covering my head; I thought I was going to die. Bullets and grape-shot showered from every direction, destroying the tree and covering me in leaves and branches.' Coignet

Between 10:30 and 12:00 noon, the Austrians attempted four major assaults on the area directly in front of Marengo and on the Courtyard itself, using fresh regiments and even eventually using their reserve of grenadiers.   Each attack failed. By about 12 noon, increasingly desperate attempts to outflank the position were made to the north and south of the main road.   To the south, this resulted in a suicidal attempt by Austrian dragoons to cross the canal in single file at a ford. It ended in disaster; the outnumbered men of the Austrian Karaczay and Kaiser dragoons were trapped and destroyed by General Kellermann's Heavy Cavalry Brigade.

To the north, the Austrians had more success. By early afternoon, pioneers had established a makeshift bridge across the ditch opposite La Borbotta farm. This allowed Austrian infantry and grenadiers to establish a bridgehead, from which they began a series of assaults on the Courtyard itself. Further north, FML Ott's 'Second Column' had also managed to negotiate the marshy ground leading to the village of Castel Ceriolo, 3km north of Marengo. With the capture of Castel Ceriolo, this 8,000-strong Column was able to move out onto the plain beyond, outflanking the French. Their advance on Marengo was, at first, contested by the three French demi-brigades of Lanne's Corps. However, eventually the Austrian advance from the north approached the Tortona road, threatening to cut off and trap the main French force at Marengo.

By 2pm, short of ammunition and under increasing pressure, the French regiments began to withdraw along their entire line. French accounts describe an ordered, strategic retreat by battalions in echelon. Austrian accounts and some more candid French memoires describe a descent into something more like a rout. Both accounts may be partly true. The French seemed to have decided to attempt a staged withdrawal. But under the pressure of sustained Austrian attacks this became, at least in places, a rout.

It was now past 2 o'clock. It was at this point that Bonaparte arrived on the battlefield. He had brought three more demi-brigades of General Monnier's division and his own Consular Guard. Victor is very clear in saying that they arrived after his decision to retreat from Marengo had already been made. Napoleon did not even attempt to defend Marengo. Instead, he used his force to screen the French withdrawal. Fearing an envelopment by Austrian troops from Castel Ceriolo, he sent the 70th, 72nd demi-brigades, the 19th Legere and the Consular Guard infantry to protect his northern flank.

One of the clearest, most perceptive eye-witness accounts is that of Joseph von Stutterheim, aide to Zach. Stutterheim claims that at this point, between 2-3pm, the Austrians began a series of attacks along their entire line. He also claims that these combined attacks finally broke French resistance and that from that moment, the French were in full retreat, if not rout.

In the centre, the Austrians had already made a series of assaults on the farm-buildings of Marengo itself, which was finally captured by Austrian Grenadiers attacking from the bridgehead at Barbotta and from a bridge near the main road constructed by their pioneers. Four successive assaults finally succeeded in capturing the Marengo courtyard, with the surrender of an entire French battalion, the 3rd Battalion of the 43rd Demi-Brigade. The capture of Marengo was the key to the battle. With the road now open, the Austrian cavalry and artillery could now move across the pontoon bridges and begin to fan out and deploy on the open plain. Once there, Austrian supremacy in guns and cavalry would begin to dominate. The cavalry in particular launched a series of charges against French infantry squares retreating along the road and plain. Almost at the same time, the Consular Guard, fighting a rearguard action, was surrounded and cut off by Austrian cavalry and infantry. Most of its 800 men were captured or killed.

The French had to retreat across a vast expanse of ground towards Cascina Grossa; a distance of at least 4 kilometres. As they retreated along either side of the road, they came under direct artillery fire both from Marengo and from Ott's Second Column in the north. They retreated for more than two hours in 30 degree heat, passing Cascina Grossa shortly after 5pm.

Austrian sources like Stutterheim, Crossard and Niepperg describe how the Austrians considered the battle won.   It is interesting that French accounts also suggest that even Bonaparte himself considered the battle lost.

"The battle seemed lost. Bonaparte, shocked and frustrated by this unexpected defeat, the first he had ever experienced, wanted to make one last desperate attempt to attack the enemy with everything he had. To either seize victory or die in the attempt. At this very point an officer galloped up at full speed to tell him that Desaix had arrived; he was already close to San Giuliano at the head of his column. At this news, his face lit up with a new look of joy and determination."
Victor.

In that time, after the destruction of the Guard, Bonaparte may have considered the grim political consequences of his defeat in Italy. However, events were to take a different, altogether unexpected, turn.

Although they had beaten the French, the Austrians had paid an extremely high price. In particular, the repeated costly assaults on the Fontanone had been mishandled, dissipating the cavalry and sacrificing the infantry.   Despite the odds, the Austrians had apparently triumphed, yet what was left of their army was in disarray. Almost all the regiments had suffered significant losses and the survivors were exhausted. They had been fighting for 6 hours in intense heat, without water. Victor estimates that both sides had lost about 8,000 men in dead and wounded in the centre alone. Most importantly, the cavalry had been dispersed and committed in piecemeal charges across the entire battlefield. Jean-Baptiste Crossard, an émigré Austrian officer, saw the victorious Austrian army quickly unravelling before his eyes.

My companion announced that victory was ours already. Yet around me there was disorder in all the ranks with soldiers running to loot the dead; everyone advanced carelessly and without order, as though they were regiments marching in peacetime. They were so busy congratulating each other or receiving congratulations, that I was shocked and taken aback by this carelessness. I called out 'We need to get into formation – our ranks need to be reformed.' I kept calling this out until I was blue in the face.
General Vogelsang, a man usually noted for his calm courteous manner, bawled back at me in anger and frustration, 'What are you shouting about? Can't you see we've got two regiments formed up and ready to advance?' Crossard

This view is echoed by every other Austrian eye-witness account. There were simply no fresh units to send against the retreating French. The losses in leadership were also appalling; over 30 senior officers and 400 junior officers were counted amongst the wounded and killed. General Melas, frail and exhausted, had also decided to retire from the field. Before returning to Alexandria, Melas gave orders that the army should continue its advance up to San Giuliano. In the heat of battle, no-one had thought to recall the 2,000 elite troopers of the 7th and 9th Hussars from their position south of Alexandria. Count von Niepperg, an officer in the Hussars, describes the situation:

'The French army was in complete disorder in this immense plain which starts at Marengo-Spinetta and borders the old Tortona road, leading to Cascina Grossa and San Giuliano. They protected their escape with some units of cavalry and infantry who made a fairly measured retreat, thanks to our slow pursuit. Apparently, this beautiful plain must have reminded us of our lovely barrack parade grounds, since our regimental bands struck up their grave and pathetic victory march, whilst our battalions took their time reforming their ranks, at leisure.' Niepperg

It took time to re-organise a new column. Sources from both sides, including Crossard, Stutterheim and General Victor estimate a period of about an hour, from 4pm to 5pm. During this time, the Austrians gathered together an advance column of two regiments and five Grenadier battalions – infantry that had suffered the fewest casualties. These units included the two Moravian (Czech) regiments, the 11th Michael Wallis and 47th Franz Kinsky. These were flanked by some regrouped dragoon regiments, principally the 3rd and 9th dragoons. By 5:30pm this advance-column marched forward along the main road, with the 47th Franz Kinsky taking a more southerly route towards Cascina Grossa; this Column was also flanked some 3km to the north by FML Ott's 'Second Column', now marching along a parallel track.

During this time, Bonaparte had ridden to meet Desaix who had already advanced past San Giuliano with his three demi-brigades. Behind Bonaparte streamed the detritus of his disintegrating army, blocking the road into San Giuliano and beyond. Officers did what they could to reform and regroup the men who remained. In doing this, they took advantage of a natural barrier of vineyards and a tree-lined road running north-south from Cascina Grossa. (See Map 3) Victor describes how Bonaparte consulted with Desaix directly over what decision to take.

'There were two courses open to us. Either we could use Desaix's new division to stop the enemy advance and then resume battle the following day or we could make one final attempt to attack and push Melas back to Alessandria. This last option was bold but its success was not impossible. An unexpected attack would be all the more effective as the Austrians were now complacent and already believed they had won a victory. Bonaparte explained all these circumstances and considerations in a manner that was very precise and lucid, whilst carelessly whipping the ground with his riding-crop. Then, he asked Desaix what he thought. Desaix who had listened to him attentively throughout, confined himself to answering, in his usual calm manner, that we still had time to win the battle. This was the answer Bonaparte wanted to hear.
Immediately, we each went back to our horses to resume our posts and staff officers were sent out in all directions to deliver the necessary orders to each unit.' Victor

What hung in the balance was Bonaparte's political career and the direction of the French republic. Desaix and all the officers present knew that Bonaparte needed a victory; nothing less would do. As such, Desaix's decision to commit his men to a counterattack was a personal commitment to Bonaparte. The counterattack, when it came involved the combined arms use of every available force left to the French. This included the army's final 18 remaining cannon, a collected remnant of 400 Heavy cavalry and dragoons and Desaix's three regiments, the 30th and 59th Ligne and the 9th Legere.

At this key point, the French outnumbered the Austrian column they were facing, for the first time that day. This was a tactic Bonaparte had used many times before in Italy; to concentrate his outnumbered troops in one area; to attack unexpectedly from a concealed position and beat the enemy at one key point. In particular, the timing and leadership of this counterattack showed the French military machine at its very best. The surprise attack was carried out from behind the tree-lined road, leading to Cascina Grossa, known today as the 'Via della Liberta.'

'It was approaching six o'clock. Our 12 piece battery hit them all at once, firing from an angle and destroying entire lines of men. The first column retreated into the second, which opened its ranks to let them pass through; this second column (of Grenadiers) closed ranks immediately and advanced resolutely with bayonets, angered by this unexpected fire. Desaix's men also advanced and both sides fired. It was at this point that Desaix was killed. Then the Light Infantry charged Lattermann's Austrian Grenadiers; the shock was tremendous. Kellerman judged this to be a decisive moment and advanced at full trot towards the enemy. When he arrived level with the enemy he commanded 'Halt!' and then 'Platoons to the left and forward!' The charge was carried out with our cavalry smashing into the flanks of Austrian battalions like lightning, one platoon after another. The enemy, attacked simultaneously by the 9th Legere, were overwhelmed and terrified, losing all cohesion. They surrendered without further resistance.' Victor

Timed to perfection, this attack destroyed the Austrian advance column, including the elite Austrian Grenadiers. Witnessing this at a distance, the Austrian cavalry which covered both flanks, suddenly took flight. In turn, their flight sparked a panic throughout the disordered ranks of the rest of the Austrian army. Niepperg describes how he saw this panic turn into a general rout.

'The cavalry fleeing at full speed, spread terror through our infantry, disordering the battalions which were placed in echelon along the length of the battlefield. As they galloped through, units of French cavalry galloped with them, penetrating our ranks. Our troops fled in the most shameful way without even firing a shot. Several battalions in the midst of the confusion and dust which surrounded them, fired at each other. The French took advantage of this to attack with their cavalry reserves, amongst whom were the Horse Grenadiers of the Consular Guard. Our cavalry disappeared on all sides and there were only a few squadrons of Bussy Light Horse who faced their attackers.
The generals and officers, who wished to show zeal and courage at such a critical moment, were either wounded or swept away by the torrent. Our soldiers rushed in crowds towards the bridgehead of the Bormida; the press became so great that neither men, nor horses, nor baggage, nor guns could pass. All were trapped; several threw themselves in the river trying to swim the distance, but were carried away by the rapidity of the current and perished.' Niepperg

To the north of the battlefield, Ott's Second Column also began its retreat, harried by French cavalry. Official French reports describe a rallying of the remaining

French troops across the entire battlefield. However, the more measured French eyewitness accounts point to an advance that was every bit as haphazard as that of the Austrians an hour earlier. With the exception of Desaix's 5,500 men, all combatants had been marching and fighting for 9 hours in intense heat, exposed to the sun and with little food or water. In a state of severe exhaustion and dehydration, they picked their way through the dead and dying that littered the battlefield, in the fading light; there would have been little room for heroics. By 10 o'clock, both armies had resumed their original positions – the Austrians at Alessandria and the French outposts at Marengo.

Marengo was a French victory in that Bonaparte had achieved his aims. He had forced the Austrians into a major battle and prevented them from re-establishing their lines of communication. More importantly, the spirit of the Austrian leadership, focused on the hapless figure of Melas, had been broken. Melas had lost most of his senior commanders, on whom he was totally dependent. The following day, he readily accepted a cease-fire agreement that would guarantee the safe passage of his army to Austrian territory. Stutterheim describes what happened at the negotiations:

'The French generals and officers, with their amiable importunity, entered the room of this weak, rest-loving old man without hesitation, yelled at him, called him a hero, a peacemaker, and feigned to admire the skill and courage with which he had pulled his army out of a difficult situation. They assured him that he had been drawn in to his difficulties through no fault of his own. They declared that Melas and Buonaparte were the first men in Europe and were solely destined to bring peace to this part of the world.
Many army officers outside the Headquarters building were suspicious of treason, even though they had no idea what might be happening. Many officers of the army, who came to the city, discussed the unexpected arrival of the French negotiators. Several were of the opinion that Berthier and his entourage should be arrested.
The peace agreement was the result of a complete exhaustion, not of the army, but of their leader, who saw only great calamity hovering over his head, without finding in his weakened body, still less in his broken spirit, the strength which one needs to face danger.' Stutterheim

The casualties told a more nuanced story. For the Austrians, Niepperg's account is a fair estimate, though probably still an under-estimate:
'According to official reports, our loss was nine thousand five hundred dead, wounded and prisoners, among whom were wounded: Lieutenant General Hadik who died of his wounds, General Comte de Bellegarde, General Lattermann,

General Vogelsang, General Gottesheim, General de Briey and General Lamarseille. These casualties also included 26 senior officers and 400 junior officers.'

The French figures are, as always, clouded by consular propaganda. However, casualty figures given by Generals Rivaud, Watrin, Lannes, Victor and Monnier for their own respective divisions amount to about 5,800 officers and men. This gives a 32% casualty rate for these divisions. If applied to the French army as a whole this would give a rough figure of 9,000 casualties. The Austrian losses based on their own official returns give a casualty rate of roughly 30%, though the true figure may have been higher.

Estimating the number of men killed or mortally wounded is even more difficult. Official returns are not reliable; both sides sought to hide negative news and there was no organised system of tracking the recovery of wounded men. Officially, the Austrians admitted to 963 men killed and the French to their usual 700, though this was later revised to 1,100. Given the high mortality rates for wounded men, these figures could safely be doubled, giving a 3-8% death rate. These are significant losses for a single day in a campaign that lasted 9 weeks. However, overall, the high losses suffered by both armies were at least comparable; at most, the battle could be judged a costly stalemate.

Warfare in the Italian Campaign of 1800

For a more general overview of the nature of Napoleonic warfare please refer to the introductory chapter in Uniforms of Austerlitz 1805 – which is intended as a companion-piece to this book.

' I am the only French officer who was present both at the siege of Genoa and at the battle of Marengo…I can hardly summon the courage to describe what the garrison and population of Genoa had to suffer during the two months this siege lasted. The ravages of famine, war and typhus were devastating. Out of 16,000 men, the garrison lost 10,000. Every day seven or eight hundred corpses of the inhabitants, of every age, sex, and class, were picked up in the streets and buried in a vast ditch filled with quicklime behind the church of Carignan. The number of victims, starved to death, reached more than 30,000. The troops alone received a miserable ration of a quarter-pound of horseflesh and a quarter-pound of a biscuit they called bread—a disgusting mix of damaged flour, sawdust, starch, hair powder, oatmeal, linseed, rancid nuts, and other nasty substances, which was bound together with a little cocoa. Each biscuit was held together with little bits of wood. In his journal General Thiebault likened it to oily peat. Rats could be bought for a high price and all the cats and dogs in the town were eaten. Typhus was rife and the hospitals were places of death.' Marbot

Five years of war and turmoil in Italy from 1795 to 1800 had seen the northern and central part of the country devastated. The country had been scoured by the continual marauding of successive armies, French, Austrian, Russian and Neapolitan. Cities had been riven by political factions and their treasuries looted. It is estimated that France extracted between 50-60 million francs in currency, precious metals and goods from Italy in the 1796-7 campaign alone.   For Republican France, campaigning in Italy was self-financing, if not lucrative. For Austria, its Italian possessions also represented a vital source of taxation and manpower.

However, maintaining armies in the Italian wars often presented an insuperable challenge.   Republican France saw successive armies fragment for want of basic provisions and ordnance.   Firstly, supplies had to be brought into French border areas often controlled by anti-Republican insurgents and organized criminal gangs; secondly, the Republican Commissariat was notoriously corrupt and inefficient; finally, once in Italy, provisions and reinforcements had to traverse mountain passes and roads or run British naval blockades.   Very little got through. This included new recruits and pay.   After months of campaigning, French armies subsisted on marauding and dressed in whatever clothes were at hand. Quite often the only standard item of uniform left was the infantry coat; the tricolore-coloured, Habit Francais. The quite often appalling state of Army of Italy troops is attested to in nearly every contemporary depiction. Mutiny, in its many forms, was commonplace. The memoires of the French Grenadier Coignet describe his own miserable state after Marengo:

'We slept on the floor on straw crawling with vermin. My breeches, waistcoat and underclothes were in a deplorable condition. In an effort to get rid of the lice which bit me constantly, I tried to boil my waistcoat and other clothes in a copper pot. Poor me. The clothes melted away and there was nothing left but the lining. There were no spare clothes in my knapsack, so I was entirely naked. My comrades helped me out. In desperation I had my friends write letters for me to my father and uncle. I begged them to send me a little money, telling them of my plight. I had to wait a long time but finally got their letters. I received both letters at the same time and had to pay for them – a franc and a half. I went to my sergeant and said, "Do me a favour and read these letters to me." He read them. My father had written, "You're too far away for me to send the money." My uncle wrote, "I can't send you anything as I've just bought some land." So much for them. I never wrote to them again in my life.'
Coignet

Although Napoleon had gone to great lengths to equip his new Army of Reserve, even an elite regiment from Paris like the 9th Legere still paraded to the Consul in Switzerland without shoes and with their uniforms in rags, on the very eve of the campaign.

Supply for the Austrian troops was easier in that they had a network of established fortified supply bases in northern Italy. Nevertheless, campaigning often took them into more mountainous marginal areas and Austrian soldiers were not trained to bivouac or maraud for their supplies. Exhaustion, malnutrition and typhus were all common blights for Austrian units on campaign. The Austrian supply system appears to have been every bit as incompetent as that of the French. The terrible conditions of soldiers arriving at Alessandria in the days before Marengo are a case in point:

Nearly always drawn from the poorest, most illiterate classes, the recruits of the Italian campaigns, from whatever nationality, had to risk disease, death and being crippled by wounds and poor medical care. Conscription did not change this. Officers fared better, depending on their rank, wealth and connections. Being seriously wounded on the battlefield was a bleak prospect for most ordinary soldiers. Horse Grenadier Petit describes the scenes in the makeshift French field hospitals:

'The next morning, overcome with hunger and deeply depressed, I entered the great court of Torre Garofoli, to look for something for myself and my horse. The sight that struck me was so horrible, I shuddered all over. More than three thousand Frenchmen and Austrians were heaped one upon another in the yard, in the granaries, in the stables and out-houses, even in the very cellars and vaults. They were uttering the most lamentable cries, mixed with threats and curses against the Surgeons; of which there were too few to dress all the wounded. Everywhere, I heard the dying voices of comrades and friends, who begged me for something to eat or drink. All that I could do was to fetch them some water. In truth, forgetting my own wants and those of my horse, I stayed there more than two hours, running backwards and forwards and performing, by turns, the job of a surgeon and hospital attendant. In short, we felt this terrible day would never end.' Petit

In 1800, the French armies of Italy were still dominated by the ideas of the French revolution, the cultural currency of the time. Although often merely rhetoric, it is undeniable that many officers still held true to ideals espoused by the Republic. Republicanism and ideas of national independence also attracted allies in nearly every Italian city. However, these cities could change their political allegiance overnight, depending on whichever army was in the ascendancy. Modena is a case in point, with city administrators changing from Republican to Austrian and back to Republican within the course of 1799-1800. Horse Grenadier Petit's entry into Milan was accompanied with outward displays of republican support:

'Everywhere the national cockade replaced the Austrian cockade. A great number of Cisalpine Refugee soldiers (from the Italian Legion) entered with us, who had been told a fortnight before of the certainty of this happy event.'

Perhaps the most pronounced aspect of the war in Italy is the way it was subject to propaganda. The 1800 campaign is no exception. The campaign was distant and far removed enough to allow official French bulletins to paint a very partial, sanitized view of events. This is even more true of the battle of Marengo, which Bonaparte desperately needed to portray as a decisive victory.

The Austrian Army in 1800

'As brilliantly as the campaign ended in 1799 with the capture of Cuneo, it had exhausted the strength of the Austrian army. The regiments had suffered much from fighting and disease, some had been reduced to 300 men, and these were lacking in many things. It is true that the greatest part of the army was transferred to winter quarters in Piedmont and the adjoining provinces of the Po valley, but only a small part on the Arno; but little was done with it. The distance from the countries from which help and reinforcements were to come to the army was great, and what happened in this respect was limited on the one hand by the limited resources, but on the other hand also by the manner in which the then Minister, Baron Thugut, and the High Command who were in charge of the Hofkriegsrat at that time, saw the needs of the army and believed they had to cover them. From this it can be explained that in the month of March, 1800, the army was only very slightly stronger than three months earlier at the end of the campaign of 1799.' Stutterheim

The Austrian Army of Italy was composed of regiments that, with few exceptions, had been fighting and campaigning in Italy for two years. During this time, they had successfully defeated French armies in two successive campaigns. By June 1800, faced with yet another invading French army and cut off from its supplies and communications, they were operating at the limits of their capacities. It was in this weakened state, that they faced Bonaparte's Army of Reserve at Marengo. Nevertheless, in terms of manpower, it still dwarfed the French in Italy.

The total forces available to the Emperor in Italy in March 1800 amounted to 101,479 men of which 86,938 were infantry and 14,541 were cavalry. After garrisons had been withdrawn and 30,000 men had been left to guard the Alpine passes, Melas was left with an army of 50,000 men to advance into the Apennines.
Stutterheim

However, this army had never fully recovered from the very intense campaigns of 1799. Over the winter of 1799-1800, its regiments had not received the new replacements and recruits they badly needed. A more fundamental reason for this is that a decade of protracted war had all but bankrupted the Austrian Treasury, now dependant on British subsidies. Joseph Stutterheim, an aide to General Zach, describes a situation in which the administrative support for the army was no longer able to properly supply or reinforce regiments in Italy.

'In the recruiting districts of the regiments, or in the capitals of the provinces, the newly enlisted men were assembled into transports for the army, given to an officer, often a novice who was to try his hand at arms and acquire practical knowledge of the service, with no other support and sent to Italy. The commander of such a transport, often 600 or even 1000 strong, had too many jobs and not enough hands. No wonder that he lost so many recruits on this long journey. The peasants, weary of the many marches, gave little or nothing in the way of food or drink to the young soldiers; they were compelled to subsist on meagre wages, despite the fact that they marched long hours and were hungry. In Italy it was even worse. The recruit never warmed up during the march through the whole of Upper Italy, and seldom found anything to cook with and, even if he had enough money, lived off the unaccustomed cold food that he found in the market places. Overnight he was squeezed into the walls of abandoned, often destroyed monasteries or into churches. Each night he slept on rotten straw, where several others had already slept. If you add the bad food to lack of basic hygiene, nobody can be surprised that out of 100 men who were sent to the army from the Fatherland, hardly 15 arrived, as was the case with the Fröhlich regiment, which had a transport sent from Kuttenberg in Bohemia made up of 560 replacement men, of whom fewer than 70 arrived at Lucca, the regiment's winter quarters.'
Stutterheim

Moreover, Stutterheim and his colleagues were very concerned that the senior officers who had led the army in 1799 had been dispersed.

At the end of the previous campaign, the minister had already called the most insightful and enterprising generals of the Italian army, Baron Kray, Count Heinrich Bellegarde, Prince Johann Liechtenstein, Count Klenau and Sommariva; the former four to Germany, the latter to be Governor of Tuscany

In their place, the Emperor Francis II and his foreign minister Baron Thugut appointed the 73 year old General, Michael von Melas. Melas had originally turned down the appointment for obvious reasons of age and ill-health, but he was eventually appointed nonetheless. As with so many other key appointments under the Emperor Francis, he was quintessentially unsuited to the task. Melas' age meant that he was often ill and dependent on taking extended rests, often spent at spas. Far more competent younger officers like Crossard and Stutterheim were unable to understand how or why he was appointed.

'The former cavalry general Baron Melas, now the chief of the army, was an old man more than 70 years old, a good soldier, brave in himself, ahead in battle; but his bravery was by no means that which, based on mental strength and self-confidence, inspires men. In former times he was considered a good cavalry officer, who knew how to get on with his men, but by now his old age made him lazy and all he wanted was to rest.
Without intellect, without any real knowledge, he was extremely work-shy; everyone who could take on the burdens of his work was a welcome companion, leaving him at most the trouble of giving his orders with a trembling hand, the content of which he did not seem to care about at all. When the Emperor, appointed him commander-in-chief of the Italian army, neither the confidence bestowed on him nor the importance of his position, not even the couriers and news sent to him by General Kray about the hostilities, warmed his zeal to speed up the journey, which he slowly continued with his baggage in leisurely stages. Yet the minister's choice fell on him! Why? — This question is difficult to answer.'

What Stutterheim failed to appreciate was that top military appointments under Francis II had little to do with military efficacy. Foreign Minister Thugut did not want a Commander in Chief who could make decisions, but one who would represent Imperial authority. The real decision-making power was given to the Army's Chief of Staff, General-Major, Anton von Zach. At 52, Zach was a technician and strategist who had been a senior lecturer at the Austrian Military Academy in Wiener- Neustadt. Highly intelligent, Zach became the effective leader of the Army in the 1800 campaign, whilst Melas readily adopted the role of figurehead. Nevertheless, the partnership did not work. Melas was surrounded by a clique of younger officers who resented Zach's lack of battlefield experience and lower social standing.   Melas and key senior staff officers like Radetzky and De Best formed a clique that openly despised Zach, yet were unable to offer any alternative positive leadership of their own.

'I have to mention one more thing about the two main characters, Radetzky and Zach. If the former combined a gallant appearance with the air of a warrior, the somewhat pedantic exterior of the latter served as the butt of jokes for the army's youth, with the result that Zach and Radetzky eventually fell out. Colonel De Best, the senior officer on the Joint Chiefs of Staff, Zach's sworn enemy, sided with Radetzky, causing irritation and confusion among many officers. Melas was far too weak to stop this infighting.'
Stutterheim

Underpinning this toxic, divided and militarily inexperienced leadership structure was an officer corps that was considerably older than its French counterpart – the average age for Austrian generals was between 45 and 70.   Furthermore, within this aging structure, advancement and promotion was dependant on social class. Commissions were controlled by higher ranking nobility, through the 'Inhaber' system; in which each regiment had an aristocratic patron as Commander in Chief.   Commoners tended to become junior officers and stayed junior officers; illiteracy was even more widespread than in the French army and this included many junior officers.   Although undoubtedly brave, there were multiple deep social divides between the higher levels of leadership, lower levels of leadership and the common soldiers.

The one thing that provided a firm foundation of common ground for the entire Austrian military establishment was a deep-rooted conservatism.   This was very much the case in 1800.   Adherents of modernizing reform like Zach, were often the very men least likely to be able to carry it out.   The army of 1800 fought in the way it had always done throughout the preceding century.   Soldiers fired muskets in three ranks and advanced into battle with fixed bayonets, often to the accompaniment of regimental bands.   Melas' Order of the Day prior to the battle is a case in point:

'It will be a matter of moving against the enemy with concentrated forces: under absolutely no circumstances are soldiers to start skirmishing.   They must remain in closed ranks even when pursuing a fleeing enemy; an enemy which might rally and counterattack. Troops must advance with bands playing and flags flying. Music inspires courage in an attacking force…Any halt in this advance in the face of the enemy skirmishers will only give them more time to inflict casualties.'
Huffer: Quellen zur Geschichte:

Skirmishing and fighting in broken order was either discouraged or forbidden. Above all, line regiments were never trained in this form of combat. This placed the Austrians at a marked disadvantage.

Light infantry duties were often given to semi-professional irregular infantry like the Grenzer border regiments. Although tentative steps in training regular battalions of light infantry had begun in 1798, there were few light infantry units available at Marengo.

The Austrian army was much more reliant on supplies and therefore also less mobile and more vulnerable. The organization and provisioning of the army was also traditional and hierarchical. Soldiers were not trained or given opportunity to forage. Regiments marched between allocated camping grounds, carrying their rations. They convened at points where they could be fed and supplied by the provisions stock-piled at military warehouses in each garrison town. Military offensives, like that against Genoa, had to be carefully planned with set timetables. For example, the attacking force at Genoa would carry eight days rations; it would then be supplied by the British Royal Navy for the duration of the siege. However, when supplies ran out, Austrian troops coped less well than their French counterparts.

If most of the army was resistant to new ideas, the Austrian artillery and technical corps were exceptions to the rule. In many ways, the artillery was highly effective and comparatively mobile for the standards of the time. It performed exceptionally well at Marengo.

Although the appearance of Austrian troops had always been much more uniform than their adversaries, the 1800 campaign saw them in a process of reform in equipment and uniform. There had been a series of radical changes in uniform and equipment in 1798, but this had only partly come in to effect. In particular, the infantry was still uniformed much as it had been prior to 1798.

"On the field, for many years (after 1798), the army cut a very motley appearance. Helmets, hats and casquets were all being worn at the same time. It was a long time before even a semblance of uniformity appeared." Ottenfeld

The only change that had been universally adopted in Italy was the new knapsack (now worn with two shoulder straps) and the standing collar; these were easy adaptations to existing uniforms. New uniforms, including the new leather infantry helmet were beginning to be introduced in 1800.* The cavalry appear to have been significantly better equipped and are shown wearing the new uniform designs throughout late 1799-1800. Regulations specifically outlined a phased introduction of new uniforms and equipment, for financial reasons. Bottom of the pile were the Grenzers and garrison battalions; written plans for the new uniform reforms specified that these secondary troops were to receive only old-pattern, reconditioned uniforms.

The Austrian Army of Italy of June 1800, was one in which morale and manpower had been sapped by two years of constant, indecisive warfare. It was in dire need of a rest and thorough refit, if not reform. In this state, the Austrian High Command were unwilling to commit it to a major battle, unless circumstances and odds appeared to be overwhelmingly in their favour. This set of circumstances would be unlikely and exceptional; yet the battlefield of Marengo on 14th June 1800 appeared to offer this very opportunity.

1800 is the first year in which prints show the new 1798 helmet being worn alongside later versions of the felt casquet.

Figure 1: Fusilier: 63rd Regiment 'Erzherzog Josef': Leib Battalion: Main Column: Fieldmarshal-Lieutenant Kaim: Initial attacks on Marengo

'The Austrian army proudly advanced on to this new battleground. Haddick's regiments were in the first line, Kaim's regiments in the second and finally a reserve column of 3,000 Grenadiers commanded by Lattermann. Further behind were a vast host of cavalry squadrons which were already forming up, shaking the earth. The whole scene was enveloped in whirlwinds of bluish smoke which vomited forth fire and iron from the cannon and howitzers ranged before it.'
Victor

An Austrian infantry regiment in 1800 consisted of two main battalions and a third battalion, often acting as a depot unit. Official strengths varied between 2,000 and 4,500 men, but the depleted regiments at Marengo fielded considerably less. The two main Battalions in a regiment were designated the 'Leib' or Guard Battalions and the 'Oberst' or Colonel's Battalion respectively; each was subdivided into 6 fusilier companies. In addition, the regiment also had a 'division' of Grenadiers subdivided into two companies; these were usually attached to composite Grenadier Battalions which fought as separate units. Each regiment had a smaller company servicing the regiment's 'Battalion Guns' which comprised both trained specialist artillerymen and supporting infantrymen. In Italy, these guns were usually small 3-pounders, with larger guns being reserved for the Rhine Army regiments.

The Austrian Imperial Army

The 63rd Erzherzog Josef Regiment was originally based in Austrian controlled Belgium where it had its recruiting area in the early 1700s. Since 1799, the entire regiment, including its depot battalion, had been based in Italy. Its fusiliers were now recruited from Bohemia and Moravia.

Brigaded under General Kaim with the 23rd Regiment Toscana, its 1,100 men were committed early on in the battle to the series of attacks on the French front-line at Marengo from about 11am until about 2pm. Like all the regiments involved in the morning attack, the 63rd suffered high casualties attempting to cross the Fontanone ditch. The infantry committed to this attack totalled five regiments backed by two divisions of Grenadiers. They barely outnumbered the defending French. As the French were steadily reinforced throughout the day, both infantry forces numbered about 13,000 men. Joseph Stutterheim, aide to General-Major Zach, describes how the first attack was made:

'General Hadik, at the head of the Bellegarde Brigade, attempted the first assault on the ditch and on the Courtyard of Marengo, which he had previously shelled. This assault was one of the bloodiest seen in this war.
The trench was reached under the heaviest fire. The courage of the Austrian infantry did not measure its depth, nor heed the resistance of the defender. However, in the face of these combined obstacles, the Austrians finally had to withdraw. It was during this attack that their brave leader, General Hadik was tragically killed by a musket ball. Large groups of enemy infantry had already arrived in force, defending the swampy deep ditch with their artillery and small arms fire. General Kaim's men then repeated the attack several times, but to no avail.'
Stutterheim

These five attacking fusilier regiments (including the 63rd) then fanned out either side of the road, in an effort to attack the French across a broader front. By the early afternoon, the 63rd were the first regiment to successfully cross and establish a bridgehead, opposite La Borbotta farm, several hundred metres to the north of Marengo. It had taken two hours of fighting to achieve this:

'The rumble of cannon and musket fire continued uninterrupted at Marengo and along the Fontanone Ditch. Both sides fought at extremely close quarters and in some places there was nothing to separate them except for a ditch some 7 metres wide (4 fathoms). Whole rows of dead and wounded were stretched out on either side of this ditch. Meanwhile a small company of Erzherzog infantry had managed to cross the ditch and capture some ground, covered in scrub and hedges, opposite La Borbotta Farm. General La Marseille brought all his

artillery to support these brave men. This enabled our Pioneers to construct a few footbridges in this area, under heavy fire and with much sacrifice.'
Stutterheim

The fusilier Regiments at Marengo were meant to wear the new 1798 uniform. However, only elements of it had been introduced. The new uniform consisted of a shortened white coat, with the tails, cuffs, collar and shoulder straps being in the regimental colour. Turn-backs did not extend all the way to the back of the coat but only as far as the two vertical side pockets. The pockets were piped in the regimental colour, as were 3 vertical seams on the rear of the coat. The coat had 10 buttons on the front and two on each cuff.

Elements of the new regulations which could be introduced by simply modifying existing equipment had been adopted early on. In particular, a broad 3-inch cross-belt for the cartridge box went over the left shoulder and the thinner 2-inch buckled belt for the bayonet scabbard went over the right. The 1800 cartridge box was large, almost the size of the knapsack. Fusiliers did not carry a short sword, apart from NCOs and musicians. A small calfskin knapsack secured by shoulder straps and a rolled greatcoat completed the equipment. A round wooden waterbottle was carried on a leather strap to the left of this knapsack. Although from sources, it appears that the older cylindrical metal canteens continued to be used as well. Black gaiters were fastened to the lower edge of the breeches. The Austrian army followed uniform-regulation more strictly than its French counterparts, even in the field.

However, contemporary prints and paintings show that important elements of the pre 1798 uniform were retained throughout 1799-1800. Most significant was the casquet; a leather and felt cap with a high front. It is commonly shown with a brass plaque bearing the Imperial eagle design. An alternative plaque design on earlier uniforms bore the FII imperial cypher (shown inset). A national yellow and black pompom was worn on the left of the casquet, together with the feldzeichen (sprig of leaves) worn on campaign. Other elements of the old pre-1798 uniform were also retained. These include plaques on fusilier cartridge cases and full buckles on bayonet cross-belts. By mid-1800, sources begin to show fusiliers wearing both the casquet and the new helmet, with the casquet still being predominant.* The military queue, a plaited pigtail, was mandatory for all infantry until it was abolished in 1804. It was 5 inches long for parade but often longer on campaign and was bound in black cloth as shown in figure 2.

The standard musket was either the 1774 or 1784-pattern musket (see Figure 3 inset), both similarly about 150cm in length with steel fittings. Although they could be loaded and fired more quickly than the French Charleville muskets, they were heavier, less accurate and less easy to maintain. Target-fire was not important in the Austrian army, as the musket was seen as a weapon of massed volley fire.   For example, fusiliers were given less than ten live-cartridges a year for target practise. At Marengo, many recruits may have been firing live rounds for the first time. The bayonet remained a primary weapon and measured just over 30 cm in length.

Regimental Colours of the Austrian Regiments at Marengo

Main Column

63rd Erzherzog Josef	Light Brown Facings	Yellow Buttons
23rd Toscana	Poppy Red Facings	White Buttons
52nd Erzherzog Anton (Hungr).	Pompadour pink	Yellow
53rd Jellacic (Hungarian).	Pompadour pink	White
11th Michael Wallis	Pink	White
47th Franz Kinsky	Steel Green	White

Northern 'Second' Column

51st Splenyi (Hungarian).	Dark Blue	Yellow
57th Colloredo.	Mauve	Yellow
28th Frohich.	Grass Green	White
40th Mittrowsky.	Carmine	White
18th Stuart.	Pompadour Pink	White
17th Hohenlohe.	Light Brown	White

(*Rugendas' 1800 print showing the siege of Cadibona in April 1800 shows both the casquet and the new leather helmet being worn by fusiliers. All earlier 1799 prints of Austrian and Hungarian fusiliers show only casquets.)

Figure 2: Grenadier: 47th   Regiment 'Franz Kinsky':   Weissenwolf Battalion attached to General-Major Weidenfeld's Grenadier Division: Main Column: Initial attacks and final rear-guard defence.

'As we advanced, General Vogelsang called out to me, 'Do you see the high morale of our men! I doubt Bonaparte will get out of this one! We've got 40,000 men, the best cavalry and complete superiority in artillery."
Crossard

The Austrians had also marshalled their best infantry, the grenadiers. Although the 47th regiment was brigaded with the 63rd in the attacks on Marengo, their grenadiers had been attached to a separate Grenadier Battalion composed of grenadiers from 3 other regiments. This was the standard practice in the Austrian army. This effectively meant that grenadiers from nearly every Austrian regiment in Italy were present at Marengo. The Weissenwolf Battalion was part of General-Major Weidenfeld's Division of just over 2,000 grenadiers.   Together with a second Grenadier Division of similar strength under General-Major Lattermann, these grenadiers were also heavily committed to the attack on Marengo.   Towards the end of the day, Weidenfeld's Division fought a rear-guard action, helping to ensure the escape of the fleeing army across the Bormida river. The Austrian Military Journal report describes these events:

'Night had arrived and the flight continued in disorder as far as Marengo. The officers made vain attempts to re-establish order and rally the men behind the line of the Fontanone; the soldiers were deaf to their orders and crowded towards the bridgehead. Infantry, cavalry, artillery and wagons all vied with each other to push through to the bridge, in a mass. They fought each other to escape. Blocked by the crowds and desperate to escape, a soldier of the Artillery Train attempted to cross the Bormida with his limber and gun and luckily succeeded in reaching the opposite bank. Others immediately followed his example; but the soft mud of the river bed could not support their weight. Very soon, 20-30 guns together with their limbers were stranded or lost in the river.

It took a long time for this mass of fugitives to pass Weidenfeld's grenadiers, and still the French did not appear. General Kellermann had called off the pursuit in order to allow the French infantry to catch up. However, they soon approached Marengo, where our grenadiers had taken up position. Our grenadiers had waited for O'Reilly's troops who were retreating from Frugarolo to the south. At Marengo, Weidenfeld's grenadiers received the French with heavy musket fire and an artillery barrage, halting their advance. In the meantime, General O'Reilly retreated along the banks of the Bormida, without any difficulty. However, once he reached the area directly behind Marengo, he began to come under sustained attack. His Croat troops blocked the enemy advance in this area, ensuring it did not reach the area of the bridgehead.

Osterreichische Militarische Zeitschrift Report

The 47th Franz Kinsky regiment were part of the large Bohemian (Czech) contingent in Melas' army. Five out of the twelve infantry regiments present at the battle were Bohemian.   The strengths of all these regiments had been significantly depleted. Although each regiment was supposed to have about 300 grenadiers, the Grenadier Companies at Marengo had barely half that number. Nevertheless, grenadiers were elite troops, given the best resources and also the most difficult tasks.

Grenadiers were identified by their bearskin hats. The back of the Austrian bearskins was cut away and covered by a cloth bag, usually striped in the regimental colour. The brass plate on the bearskin had a crowned imperial eagle design; the bearskin fur was usually oiled and swept upwards. A national yellow and black pompom was worn on the right, attached to which was a sprig of feldzeichen. Other grenadier distinctions included a brass match-holder attached to the cartridge box crossbelt and a brass grenade-badge attached to the cartridge box itself. Grenadiers also carried a 79cm long sabre on the same cross belt as the bayonet. This was a formidable weapon. (see inset Fig.5)

Regimental Colours of Grenadier Companies at Marengo*

The list below gives the number, facing colour and button colour of the regimental grenadier companies forming each battalion. 51:Darkblue:Y denotes the 51st Regiment: Dark blue facings: Yellow buttons.

General-Major Lattermann's Grenadier Brigade   2,220 men
- Parr Hungarian Battalion 51:Darkblue:Y   52: Pompadour:Y
- St Julien Battalion   18:Pompadour:W   17: Light Brown:W   24:Darkblue:W
- Schiaffinati Battalion   28:Green:W   40:Carmine:W   63:Lightbrown:Y
- Kleinmayer Battalion   4:Skyblue:Y   10:ParrotGreen:W   13:Green:Y
- Weber Battalion   45:Red:Y   55:Lightblue:Y   59:Orange

General-Major Weidenfeld's Grenadier Brigade   2,520 men
- Khevenholler Batt.   26:Green:Y   27:Yellow
- Pieret Battalion   8:Red:Y   44:Madder:W   46:Darkblue:Y
- Pertusi Hungarian Batt.   19:Lightblue:W   34:Madder:W   39:Red:
- Perss Hungarian Batt.   48:Steel Green:Y   32:Lightblue:Y   35:crabred:Y
- Gorschen Hungarian Batt. 33:Darkblue:W   53:Pompadour:W
- Weissenwolf Battalion   11:Pink:W   23:Red: W   47:Steel Green:W

The list above is a tentative summary of the Grenadier companies forming Weidenfeld's and Lattermann's two Grenadier Brigades, based on Naufziger's order of battle and other sources. However, these grenadier battalions were often ad hoc units which changed their composition and officers according to needs and circumstances. There is no reliable source detailing their composition. Furthermore, it is possible that one or more of the Hungarian Grenadier battalions in Weidenfeld's brigade were attached to Lattermann's brigade as part of the Advance Column in the early evening.

The exact pattern of Austrian Grenadier plates varied over time. (See Fig 126 below) This example is drawn from a bearskin in a private collection. The bearskin may date to 1806. However, the plate itself may be older, as it is the pattern that features in the Mollo prints of 1798.

Austrian Grenadier Bearskin Plates

48   The Austrian Imperial Army

Figure 2

Figure 1

49   The Austrian Imperial Army

Figure 3

Figure 3: Grenadier Corporal: 23rd Regiment 'Toscana': attached to General-Major Weidenfeld's Grenadier Division: Main Column: Initial attacks on Marengo

The Grenadiers of the 23rd Toscana Regiment were detached from their parent regiment and formed part of Weidenfeld's Grenadier Division (see article on Fig. 2 above). The 23rd Toscana was the only German speaking regiment present at Marengo, being recruited from hereditary lands in Austria. This same regiment was to play a central role at the battle of Austerlitz 5 years later; although by then it was renamed the 23rd 'Salzburg'. At Marengo, the whole regiment was committed early on, to the assaults on the courtyard of Marengo itself. The courtyard dominated the main Tortona road, and the Austrians needed to capture it. From about 1pm to 2:00pm, they carried out 4 attempts to storm the courtyard, crossing by two pontoon bridges, one at the road and another opposite Borbotta farm. By about half past two, the courtyard had been captured and the Tortona road was opened for a general advance by the entire army;

'General Lattermann now crossed over the catwalk bridges with his grenadiers and again tried to take the Courtyard of Marengo by storm. Meanwhile, Major Perzel of the artillery, was shelling Marengo with his reserve batteries, having previously silenced the French artillery stationed there. However, the French General Rivaud was able to repel this assault, bringing up reinforcements. During these attacks, General Lattermann, commander of our grenadiers was wounded.
Meanwhile, General Bellegarde had brought several detachments of Hungarian infantry over the catwalk bridges. These fresh troops resumed the assault together with the grenadiers, and finally succeeded in capturing and holding the courtyard. The inner courtyard of Marengo and the ground around it was covered with dead. After a bloody resistance, some 400 French troops surrendered there. We had captured 10 guns, 2 howitzers and about 3,000 prisoners. The battlefield was covered with dead and wounded; General Bellegarde was amongst the wounded. I had never witnessed a French army in such a state of disarray. By capturing the court of Marengo, the bridge on the military road to Tortona was cleared, and the main body of the army was able to cross unhindered.'
Stutterheim

Figure 3 is a Corporal of Grenadiers. Austrian Corporals were senior NCOs, equating to Sergeants in most other armies. He wears the new 1798 uniform in its entirety. His Grenadier uniform carries the Imperial eagle brass plaque, worn at the time; a brass matchcase is attached to his cartridge box belt and the box itself is marked with a brass grenade badge. The cross-belt for the bayonet and sabre has a standard new 1798 half-buckle. His distinctions of rank include a cane, stirrup hilt sabre, woollen yellow-black sword knot and gloves. He is armed with the newer 1784 pattern musket, which he would not have carried on formal parades. The musket and bayonet stood at 180cm in length, the standard height for a grenadier. The Grenadiers of the 23rd Toscana survived Marengo to be destroyed five years later, at Austerlitz; over-run by the cuirassiers of the Grand Armee.

Figure 4: Fusilier: 57th Regiment 'Colloredo': Oberst Battalion: Second Column: Fieldmarshal-Lieutenant Ott: Advance on Castel Ceriolo in the northern part of the battlefield.

Figure 5: Hungarian Fusilier 'Gefreiter' Corporal: 51st Regiment 'Splenyi': Oberst Battalion: Second Column: Fieldmarshal-Lieutenant Ott: Advance on Castel Ceriolo in the northern part of the battlefield.

The 57th and 51st were two of the six regiments that formed Ott's Second Column advancing from Castel Ceriolo, 3km to the north of Marengo. The 1,300 strong 57th was yet another Bohemian (Czech) regiment. All six regiments had fought at the battle of Casteggio-Montebello 5 days before Marengo, suffering significant losses. The Second Column had great difficulty travelling the winding 4km route to Castel Ceriolo, a secondary route which followed the course of the river. It took them about 3 hours to travel along the mud track (marked as the Chemin de Pavie on the map above) crossing both the Fontanone and a secondary canal along the way. The Austrian officer, Crossard, describes their difficulties:

The Austrians advanced along their left (northern) flank, but their success was hindered by a series of obstacles. In that area, we had to approach Castel Ceriolo, crossing difficult terrain. Our troops followed a track that wound through marshy ground; either side of which were thickly planted vineyards. These obstacles deprived us of the quick movement necessary for the outflanking manoeuvre we had in mind.
Crossard

Nevertheless, by early afternoon the six regiments of Second Column had captured Castel Ceriolo and pushed back the right wing of the French army. Even in this northern area of the battlefield, the 7,500-strong Austrian infantry did not significantly outnumber the five French demi-brigades eventually sent to oppose them. Stutterheim describes their hard-fought advance:

General Ott's Second Column were the last to cross the Bormida bridge. They made their way along a narrow track which wound through scrubland towards Castel-Ceriolo. The village was only weakly held by the French who retreated upon our first assault. The French retreated north towards Sale and we had them pursued by our Lobkowitz dragoons who took a number of prisoners. The French concerned for their right (northern) wing sent one demi-brigade against us which succeeded in capturing a few houses at the entrance of the village. However, our troops soon forced them out. As we exited the village, we entered an open plain which stretched from Marengo to San Giuliano; henceforth we were able to advance unhindered.
Stutterheim

The 51st Splenyi regiment was one of three Hungarian regiments at the battle, together with several Hungarian grenadier companies. Hungarian infantry had gained a reputation for bravery, with recruits drawn from a region that included both Croats and Transylvanians (Romanians). This was definitely true of the 51st Splenyi, a Transylvanian regiment. Nick-named 'Hell's Legion', intense fighting over preceding days had more than halved the effective strength of the 51st to just over 700 men. Despite this, at Marengo, it engaged the Consular Guard in a drawn-out firefight, firing volleys in line, before attacking it with a bayonet charge. Stutterheim continues his account:

As our men advanced through a slight depression in the ground, they saw a column approach them. Advancing through a field of high-standing wheat, they could see tall red plumes, the mark of the Consular Guard. General Ott, on seeing them, hastened to form up the Lobkowitz Light Dragoons. However, a volley of musket fire by the Guards disordered its ranks and they fled, pursued in turn by French cavalry. At this point, a battalion from the Splenyi regiment broke ranks and charged the enemy cavalry with bayonets; this cavalry also turned and fled. After this, General Gottesheim was ordered to form up the Splenyi regiment together with one battalion of the 28th Frohlich and attack the Consular Guard. Both opposing forces formed up in line, firing volley fire at each other for some time, as if on a parade ground.
Stutterheim

The fire-fight with the Consular Guard took place at some time after 2pm. In the meantime, Marengo had been captured which allowed a large group of Hungarian hussars to outflank the Guard and attack it from the rear. Attacked from all sides, the Guard was over-run with most of the survivors surrendering. Stutterheim completes the account:

The rolling volley fire against the Guard continued even after fighting at Marengo had ceased; Gottesheim was badly wounded. General Vogelsang (with the 18th

Stuart and 17th Hohenlohe) was also similarly engaged with the demi-brigades of General Cara-St-Cyr (the 70th DB and 19th Legere). At this moment, several squadrons of 8th Nauendorf Hussars and Bussy Light-Horse rushed up along the road leading from Marengo and charged the Guards from the rear. This was a decisive attack, putting an end to all fighting and resistance in the area. Many of the Consular Guard were killed outright and most of them surrendered and were captured together with their four cannon. The French have so far kept this a secret. I, the author, was present and witnessed the entire action. I invite any member of the Consular Guard who was present at Marengo to challenge my account; an account which does them no dishonour. Shortly after this event, some officers of the Guard in Milan told me that hardly 100 of them remained; though after we released our prisoners, their number reached 500 once more.
Stutterheim

Hungarian fusiliers were uniformed like other Austrian infantry, apart from distinctive woollen Hungarian trousers; light blue with black and yellow lace decorative knots and outer seams. The split cuffs of their coats were also marked by a distinctive lace decoration called baretzen; a double strip of white lace fixed by either one or two buttons. Laced ankle-length boots replaced the shoes and gaiters of other Austrian fusiliers.*

This Hungarian fusilier still has the old brass imperial eagle plaque on his cartridge box. His casquet has a rear peak, often shown in visual sources of infantry on the march (e.g prints of an Austrian patrol by Bleuler or prints by Suhr); infantry in marching order are also often shown wearing their casquet turned back to front, with this rear-peak shielding their eyes. Kobell's painting of a group of infantry and uhlans in 1800 also shows one figure with a peak attached to the front of his casquet – though this was unusual.

Figure 5 also carries the distinctions of non-commissioned rank as a Gefreiter – a Junior Corporal: distinctions include a cane and an infantry sabre. A full-strength fusilier company of 230 men usually had 16 NCOs, which were headed by a Feldwebel and a Fourier but also included Corporals, Gefreiters and a Sapper. These men provided both leadership and also a core of professional competency, amongst soldiery that often had only the most rudimentary training.

The **Austrian 1780-pattern infantry sabre** was a long weapon, with a 67cm blade and a full length of 79cm. Later versions would be shortened but in 1800, this was the standard length. It was supplied to NCOs and to Grenadiers, having at least 3 different types of pommel (see inset) – pommels with guards and lion head decorations were reserved for higher ranks. The blade was always of a similar pattern bearing the FII cypher and imperial eagle stamp with two crowns.

54   The Austrian Imperial Army

55 The Austrian Imperial Army

Figure 7

Figure 6

Three surviving examples of scabbards are in dark leather, ending smoothly in a simple brass chape**
The fusilier from the 57th Colloredo regiment in Figure 4 wears the full new pattern uniform, including new leather helmet and new cartridge box without a brass plaque. These items were only just beginning to be issued to the Army of Italy during the 1800 campaign, usually by way of new recruits. Tied to the right of his knapsack, is a hardened wooden tent peg – a regulation item.

In the Austrian army, the term 'Hungarian' included Croats and Romanians amongst others – all other national-ethnic groups, including Czechs, Slovaks, Slovenes, Poles, Ukrainians and Italians were usually referred to as 'German'.
**There is no evidence of a pronounced leather fold at the end of the scabbard – at least for this period.*

Figure 6: Hungarian Grenadier: 52nd Regiment 'Erzherzog Anton': attached to General-Major Lattermann's Grenadier Division: Main Column: Initial attacks on Marengo and advance-column at Cascina Grossa.

Figure 7: Grenadier: 28th Regiment 'Frohlich': attached to General-Major Lattermann's Grenadier Division: Main Column: Initial attacks on Marengo and advance-column at Cascina Grossa.

The twin Hungarian regiments of 52nd Erzherzog Anton and 53rd Jellacic had been the first to attempt a frontal assault on Marengo. They were also involved in the final storming of the Courtyard at Marengo. These two regiments remained heavily committed throughout the morning, sustaining heavy casualties and were no longer able to play an active role in the battle thereafter. The 28th Regiment 'Frohlich' yet another of the Czech regiments at Marengo was heavily committed in attacking the northern flank of the French position at Marengo. It fought in line, fighting off a series of French counterattacks and eventually contributing to the destruction of the French Consular Guard (see Fig. 5). However, Grenadiers from all 3 regiments appear to have been attached to General Lattermann's Grenadier Division.
The Hungarian Grenadier in Figure 6 wears a new 1798-regulation uniform, with Hungarian trousers, boots and cuff lace (see Fig. 5). The Grenadier in Figure 7 marches in a greatcoat, usually only worn in marching order. This figure shows how the knapsack was carried prior to 1798; by a single cross-belt passing over the right shoulder. This would have been an exception to the rule, as by 1800 all sources show the knapsack being carried on two shoulder straps.

By the mid-afternoon, the Austrian High Command considered the battle won. General Melas decided to retire from the field and charged General Zach with the task of pursuing the retreating French as far as San Giuliano. Zach was given two regiments, the 47th Franz Kinsky and 11th Michael Wallis as well as Lattermann's Grenadiers to carry out the task. In particular, Lejeune's painting of the final French counterattack at Cascina Grossa, shows Hungarian grenadiers in the middle and rear ranks of the pursuing column.

The units forming Zach's 'advance column' had lost their two key commanding officers – Lattermann and Haddik - both casualties. Furthermore, given the casualties sustained during the day, the two regiments and 4 battalions of grenadiers, cannot have numbered more than 3,000 infantry. To the north of the old road, they were flanked by the remnants of the 63rd and 23rd infantry regiments; adding perhaps another 1-2,000 infantry. Many of these troops had been fighting in intense heat for over 7 hours. All Austrian accounts state that even the forward column marched in a state of considerable disorder. Stutterheim describes an army in a state of near exhaustion.

Our middle or main Column now followed the French across this wide open plain, in some disarray. For cavalry, we had the 3rd Erzherzog Johann and the 9th Lichtenstein; two regiments that had not been heavily engaged thus far and who had established a good reputation in previous campaigns. For infantry, we had the 11th Michael Wallis regiment and 4 battalions of grenadiers, units that had suffered least in the fighting so far. They were led by General St Julien and accompanied by a couple of artillery batteries. They were surrounded by swarms of skirmishers from all regiments, who were also pursuing the enemy. This Column proceeded along the military road to San Giuliano in the direction of Torre di Garofoli. In this great heat, other units of the army had scattered to find food and water in the dwellings around Spinetta, Longofame, Poggi and Cascina Grossa. Whilst some tried to bring water to the thousands of wounded, others tried to find food. Detachments of cavalry were also sent out to find fodder and water for the horses.
Stutterheim.

Figure 8: Fusilier: 11th Regiment 'Michael Wallis': Main Column: Reserve regiment in the initial attack on Marengo and lead regiment in the Advance-Column at Cascina Grossa.

The Austrian greatcoat was made from rough woollen fabric dyed light-tan brown or grey – the cheapest dye-colours. The coat was usually knee-length or shorter, for infantry. Cavalry coats were longer and split at the front and rear, so that they could be worn on horseback. For cavalrymen, a short blanket was also carried in

58 The Austrian Imperial Army

Figure 8

Figure 9

front of the saddle. The fusilier in Figure 8 also wears a later version of the casquet; casquets worn in 1799-1800 were generally taller than those worn at the start of the decade.

The 2,200 men of the 11th Regiment 'Michael Wallis' had been kept as a reserve at the start of the battle and were still relatively unscathed when an Advance-Column was organized in the late afternoon. The regiment led this column accompanied by regimental bands, with orders to advance as far as San Giuliano. The capture of San Giuliano and its cross-roads would have seen the Austrians achieve all their battle aims.

However, sources suggest that the 11th Wallis may have advanced in marching order. In particular, Lejeune depicts Austrian troops wearing their greatcoats, items that were usually only worn on the march. This order of dress may be symptomatic of the complacent way in which the Austrians conducted their pursuit.

Figure 9: Fusilier: Piedmontese 'Alessandria' Battalion: Garrison: Garrison Reserve kept at Alessandria.

There were at least four Piedmontese units garrisoned at Alessandria, fulfilling the important role of guarding the rear of the Austrian army. Three of these battalions arrived the day before the battle: the Turin, Asti and Casale Battalions. At the end of the day, they formed the only remaining cohesive units at the Bormida bridgehead.

A single battalion of the garrison of the citadel manned the bridgehead. This battalion succeeded only with the greatest difficulty in maintaining some semblance of order. An officer, I can't remember who, was shouting to all the fugitives that they should follow an order of the General-in-Chief; each battalion was to reassemble on the banks of the Bormida, in the camps allocated the previous day. This act greatly contributed to the reorganisation of the army that took place over the course of the night.
Niepperg

The Piedmontese Army was a shadow of what it had been in the early 1790s when it successfully fought off repeated French incursions over three years of campaigning. By the late 1790s, what remained of the Piedmontese army had been partitioned between Austria and France, with individual regiments often switching allegiance to whichever major power happened to have the upper hand. Regiments were riven by divided loyalties, with the officer corps tending to owe allegiance to the exiled Piedmontese monarchy and their Imperial allies. Their value as garrison troops made Niepperg lament their loss in the treaty of Campo Formio, signed after the battle:

During the entire march (after the ceasefire) back to Austrian controlled territory, our columns were accompanied by French troops who mingled amongst our men, discussing subversive (political) ideas. The French reneged on the treaty terms and deceived us in the division of artillery and supply arrangements, so that when hostilities broke out once again, everything remained in their possession. Furthermore, this treaty caused us to lose a further 12,000 Piedmontese troops; troops that weren't mentioned in the treaty and who were summarily demobilized.
Niepperg

Figure 9 is based on a contemporary watercolour by Rovatti who painted the Alessandria Regiment during 1799 when it was still controlled by the French. The fusilier wears a French style uniform based on a dark blue coat with orange facings. Each Piedmontese regiment had different coloured facings. Two cross-belts carried a cartridge box and a bayonet/short-sword respectively. The fusilier also wears a white, black and blue cockade; this item is quite possibly the only thing that was discarded when the regiment switched allegiance to the Austrians in mid-1799. The Rovatti drawings also include Piedmontese cavalry regiments, dressed similarly to French Heavy Cavalry.

THE AUSTRIAN ARTILLERY

Figure 10: Vormeister Gun-Commander: Battalion Guns of 28th Regiment 'Frohlich': Ott's Second Column in the northern part of the battlefield.

Figure 11: Feuerworker: Major Perzel's Cavalry Artillery Battery: Main Column.

These Austrian Columns were not covered by a cloud of skirmishers as was the usual custom; instead, they were preceded by a strong force of artillery and this force advanced at a rapid, decisive pace, determined to pass over the dead bodies of all who stood in its path.
Victor

Austria's artillery were still considered to be the most advanced and best trained in Europe. At Marengo, they more than proved it, gaining an unchallenged supremacy over the battlefield and acting as an advance force for the army as a whole. The Austrians started the battle with an overwhelming superiority in guns, yet their artillery also displayed a high level of aggressive proficiency.

61   The Austrian Imperial Army

Figure 11

Figure 10

They were equipped with over 80 cannons in total, with possibly half this number being heavier cannon used by at least 8 Cavalry and Reserve Batteries; each Cavalry Battery was usually equipped with four 6-pounder cannon and two howitzers. The 6-pounder cannon were particularly prized, being as powerful as the French heavy 8-pounders, but much lighter and more manageable. Another 40 or so small 3-pounder cannons were dispersed amongst the infantry regiments and used as Battalion-guns.

The Austrian Artillery Colleges could be rivalled only by those in France, prior to the revolution. The artillery was the only branch of the army that was almost exclusively German speaking; it had to be. Cannoneers had to be literate and anyone aspiring to officer status had to undergo 7 years of practical and theoretical study. Completion of 5 years or under would only qualify the cadet for a non-commissioned role, which might yet lead to officer status. The important tactical unit was the 'Company Battery' of about 150-200 men, usually with batteries of six guns and howitzers. Regiments were merely the administrative entities for these Companies.

Once the recruit entered a Company, he entered a rigidly stratified world of 1st class gunners (Cannoneers), 2nd class gunners (untercannoniers) and Handlager (Gunhandlers). When the guns were unlimbered, most untercannoniers and Handlager performed their secondary role to protect the guns; as such they were armed with carbines and cartridge cases. Each Company Battery had 6 guns and 15-20 limbers and caissons. Within each gun-team, roles would include; rammer, munitioner, firer, charger, aimer and commander. At Marengo, the artillery was divided between regimental 'Battalion Guns', mobile Cavalry-Batteries and heavier Reserve Batteries.

Figure 10 shows a Gun-Commander of the Battalion Gun company for the 28th Regiment 'Frohlich'. This was one of the very few regiments partly equipped with heavier 6 pounders; cannons that would be used against the Consular Guard in the late afternoon. Battalion Guns were usually light half-batteries of 3-pounders, with 6-pounders being rare exceptions; these guns were usually operated by specialist Cannoneers, but supported by a trained detachment of infantrymen appointed from the regiment. The 3-pounders used by Battalion Guns were very small light-cannon, used for firing grapeshot at close range. At Marengo, they were used to deadly effect when supporting infantry, often making up for the deficiencies in Austrian musketry. Grapeshot fire from a 3-pounder was similar to short, sudden bursts of machine-gun fire and these small cannons enabled the Austrians to outgun the French infantry throughout the day. Handled by an expert team, light cannon could also fire small golf-ball sized

The Austrian Imperial Army

round shot with extreme accuracy. Furthermore, as Austrian artillerymen considered themselves an elite; it was dangerous to under-estimate them. In an engagement earlier in the 1800 campaign, the young hussar Marbot discovered this to his expense:

We were falling back towards our own troops without having encountered the enemy, when our officer Pertelay spotted an enemy battery of 8 guns on the extreme left flank of the enemy line. This battery was causing severe casualties to our infantry. With unpardonable impudence, this Austrian battery had advanced seven or eight hundred feet in advance of its own infantry regiment, in an effort to improve its aim. It was positioned on a little rise and the commander of the battery evidently thought that with a perfect view of the entire French front line he would be able to see any force sent to attack him; he could then simply fall back to his own lines before it arrived.
Marbot

The Austrian gunners, particularly those of the Cavalry-Battalions were trained to bring their guns very close to enemy formations. However, Marbot's squadron managed to attack this particular battery from the cover of a nearby wood. They consequently captured 6 guns and their limbers, leaving two behind still in possession of the artillerymen. This was a fatal mistake.

Although we had no choice to leave the two guns behind, this decision resulted in the death of our commander. No sooner had we left with our captured guns, than the gunners and their officers returned to the two remaining guns. They had been taking cover under the ammunition wagons, protected from our swords. They loaded the cannons with canister and fired at our backs. You can readily see that we presented a wide and easy target; 30 troopers, with 6 guns, each harnessed to 6 horses and driven by 3 drivers. Every ball hit its mark. We had two sergeants and several hussars killed or wounded as well as one or two of the drivers; several horses were also maimed so that the limbers could make no further progress… Just as we were about to reach our own lines, the enemy changed to using round-shot and fired two cannon-balls, one of which killed poor Pertelay, hitting him in the kidneys.
Marbot

Figure 11 shows a Fireworker, a senior NCO, of the Cavalry Battery supporting the Austrian Main Column attack on Marengo. He wears a short artillery greatcoat. Austrian 'Cavalry Batteries' were mobile units, usually servicing much more powerful 6-pounders, firing both grapeshot and solid shot. The 6-pounder gun carriages were designed with long thin leather seats. Most of the gun team rode into battle astride these seats, pulled by a 6-horse limber. Other members of the team followed on the caisson, which was also designed as a long, thin seat. The sausage-shape of these vehicles earned them the title 'wurst' wagons. The system allowed a trained gun-team to dismount, unlimber and fire a gun in seconds:

Our cavalry cannon halts; the commands `Halt!` `Dismount!` `Front!` `Gun commander fire!` are given almost without a pause and are as rapidly executed. The gunners jump off even before the horses have stopped; the gun carriage is unhooked from the limber and turned to face the enemy as the limber goes to the rear; the cartridge is loaded and the first shot is fired.
Baron Karl Smola, OberLieutenant in the Austrian Artillery. Translated by: Digby G. Smith, Thetford, 2010.

The 6-pounder batteries at Marengo focussed on counter-battery fire; trying to destroy the French artillery. Horse Grenadier Joseph Petit described how they achieved this with deadly efficiency:

The enemy were served by thirty guns which sliced both men and trees in two. Shattered branches splintered and fell on our men and on the wounded who had taken refuge underneath, crushing them to death. Our own artillery had been either destroyed, captured or had run out of ammunition. In short, I have no hesitation in saying that by 4 o'clock in a front line covering more than 5 miles we had no more than 6 French cannon and less than a thousand men, still by their colours.
Petit

The Austrian artillery coat was usually wolf-grey – a mixed grey and red-brown fabric, though contemporary prints show a range of uniform variations and colour-pigments from brown to faded grey; often within the same gun team. One print by Seele (datable to this period) of a Battalion-Gun Battery shows every one of the 5 artillerymen wearing a slightly different uniform – including a supporting handlager wearing a standard fusilier uniform.

The coat facings for the artillery were red and there were straps edged in red on each shoulder. For this period, breeches could be white or wolf-grey and were worn with short gaiters. Artillerymen wore three 2-inch cross-belts. Two passing over the right shoulder for the artillery short sword and the rolled greatcoat-sack (also wolf-grey) and one passing over the left shoulder for a holster-shaped port-fire-case which contained a selection of tools and tinder. Gunners often wore their knee length greatcoats when firing the guns, to protect their uniform. Handlagers and some Cannoneers also carried a bricole on their right shoulder; a length of rope used to haul the gun, in order to advance, at walking pace.

Dress-code for artillerymen and engineers required them to be clean shaven with no moustaches though the military queue was still mandatory. Head-dress throughout the period included the plain round-hat for 'other ranks' and bicorns for officers and senior NCOs, often edged in yellow or gold galloon-ribbon. Some NCOs continued to wear round-hats and Seele shows one wearing a round-hat edged with gold ribbon. One campaign, plumes were usually only worn by NCOs and are shown black with a large yellow band. These could be attached to a yellow and black pompom either to the side, but more usually to the back of the round-hat. The bicorn and round-hats worn in this period were markedly different to the tall, flat cross-sectioned bicorns and corsehuts worn after 1808. Artillerymen also carried a shortened version of the sabre with a guardless hilt.

Officers' distinctions were similar to that of the infantry and included; a yellow sash striped with black thread; gloves; a thicker band of gold galloon for the bicorn; and an officer's coat with long tails, also wolf-grey. The 1798 regulations also prescribed a version of the new leather infantry helmet for some artillerymen; the brass front-plate was embossed with the image of a cannon (see inset). However, there are no contemporary sources to indicate whether these helmets were ever worn or which part of the artillery wore them – although they may have been worn by artillery fusiliers assigned to protect some gun-teams.

Figure 12: Gefreiter: Mule Train company attached to Reserve Artillery: Supply Column at Bormida Bridgehead.

Supply and the organization of supplies plagued the Austrian army throughout the campaign of 1800, despite their well-stocked network of military storehouses and fortified garrison towns. Yet there had been efforts to ensure that the artillery, at least, had an organized system of transport and supply; this role fell to the specialized Artillery Transport Train.

Their duties included handling the four-horse ammunition and powder caissons and six-horse limbers for Cavalry Artillery Batteries. The 80 guns at Marengo would have been supported by an equal number of limbers and an even greater number of ammunition and powder caissons, either parked behind the regiments or stretching out along the tracks and single military road leading to the Bormida bridgehead. Only draught-horses were used to pull these vehicles on the battlefield, both for their speed and because they could be trained to not shy at gunfire. However, for transport to and from the battlefield, mule-trains were

66 The Austrian Imperial Army

Figure 12

The Austrian Imperial Army

routinely used. This was particularly the case in Italy where both pack-mules and heavier draught-mules were used to negotiate mountain passes; many of these animals would have been commandeered from the local populace. Marbot describes how important these animals were in mountainous countries;

During this time, there were very few carriage horses and all carriages were drawn by mules. For posting, there were only saddle horses, so that even the richest nobles who had their own carriages, were forced to hire mules for a day journey when they travelled. Poorer people joined caravans of donkey drivers, who transported goods. Nobody travelled alone, partly because of their fear of highwaymen.
Marbot

Artillery drivers were non-combatants and were generally unarmed. As such they usually had a military escort. All ranks wore a standard grey coat with yellow facings on the collar and cuffs; the turn-backs are sometimes shown as grey piped in yellow. They either wore grey cloth breeches or grey buttoned riding trousers – for officers these are shown with a yellow stripe on the outer seam. All drivers wore short boots and a felt round-hat, decorated with a national pompom and black over yellow plume. Officers and NCOs had silver galloon-tape on the brims and base of their hats. Drivers also wore a yellow and black armband for easy identification. Like all the artillery in general, they are always depicted clean-shaven.

Figure 13: Private: 3rd Light Infantry 'Bach' Battalion: Advance Guard: Leading the attack on Pietrabuona farm and thereafter supporting Second Column.

In action soldiers must remember not to lose time firing. Only a few sharpshooters are necessary to screen the front. If these are followed up by soldiers advancing bravely, in closed formation with bands playing, then an enemy in open order cannot repel such an advance.
Melas' instructions to the Army April 1800

There were two Light Infantry Battalions at Marengo (the 2nd 'Bach' and 4th Am Ende Battalions) with a further one (the 2nd 'Rohan' Battalion) stationed some 30 km away, towards Asti. All three were recruited in northern Italy, though a core of veterans and non-commissioned officers were drawn from German Rhineland troops; former freicorps soldiers. The Light Infantry Battalions were new units,

68 The Austrian Imperial Army

Figure 14

Figure 13

formed during the 1798 reforms, and designed to counter the French superiority in light infantry skirmishing.

Although both Battalions formed part of the 'Advance Guard' leading the attacks on Pietrabuona farm and Marengo, they were then assigned to lead Second Column's advance. From mid-morning, the 2nd 'Bach' and 4th Am Ende Battalions formed an advance skirmish line for the Austrian Second Column on the Northern flank.   The émigré officer Crossard describes how he led at least one light infantry company in counterattacking Desaix's troops towards the final stages of the battle:

'I took it upon myself to bring a company of Bach's Light Infantry to the vineyards north of the military road. The Second-Lieutenant of this company was Baron de Gaugraeber, who afterwards became a captain in Carl Shroeder's regiment.
Placed on the right flank of the enemy, its fire stopped their pursuit for a moment. This is an accurate account.   If only our action had been backed by more troops, we would have had a significant effect.   Yet far from supporting us, the other troops (of Second Column) began their retreat.'
Crossard

Both Light Battalions were also involved in the defence of Marengo on 13th June, the day before the battle; sustaining some 80 casualties.   Although armed with standard muskets, the two Battalions would also have had select marksmen armed with rifles, as in the Grenz regiments.   The adoption of light infantry units and training had already become part of a politicised conflict between pro-reform and anti-reform cliques in the Austrian High Command.   After the defeat at Marengo, the conservatives gained the upper hand and the Light Infantry units were disbanded.

Nevertheless, from 1798-1800 the light infantry feature prominently both in prints and in how they were prioritised for new uniform and equipment.   They were the first units to be issued with the new 1798 leather helmet and the new infantry coat. In essence, they wore a light-grey version of the fusilier uniform, with few other differences: most notably, light infantry helmets did not have a front brass plate, having only the FII cypher*.

The Light Infantry Uniforms at Marengo

3rd Bach Light Infantry Battalion	Dark Red facings	Yellow (buttons)
4th Am Ende Light Infantry Battalion	Dark Red facings	White
2nd Carl Rohan Light Infantry Battalion	Crab Red facings	White

*It is unclear whether this was a brass badge or merely painted on.

Figure 14: Jager: Italian-Field-Army 'Mariassy' Jager Battalion: Advance Guard: Leading the attack on Pietrabuona Farm.

The Jagers were specialist riflemen, usually recruited from the Austrian Tyrol. The preference was for game-keepers and men already practiced in marksmanship. They are always shown armed with rifles, and appear to have worked closely with light infantry units. However, the 6 companies of the Italian-Field-Army Jager Corps led by Andras Mariassy were recruited from former Piedmontese army riflemen; most of this unit was present at Marengo. As with the light infantry, this was a new unit, formed in the summer of 1799; it had already fought at Genoa. Like the Light Infantry battalions, this Jager unit was also disbanded shortly after 1800. They appear to have served in small company-sized units, attached to the Advance Guard, to Ott's Second Column and to Third Column. Niepperg describes how it was a unit of Jagers and light infantry together with 63rd fusiliers, who managed to secure a bridgehead opposite Borbotta

In this area, we forced back the enemy and some of our skirmishers crossed the canal over planks; supported by two battalions of the 63rd Erzherzog Joseph, they occupied the buildings and mill beyond. They held this position for some time. However, the pioneers took time bringing up their small pontoon bridges (Laufbrucken) as the traffic on the Bormida bridge prevented them from crossing. We searched for these small bridges but could not find them. Therefore, it seemed imprudent to bring more men into this bridgehead, which was still unsupported and surrounded by enemy troops.
Niepperg

The Jager uniform was based on a grey version of the standard infantry coat, with green facings. The jager infantry helmet also had a black-over-green woollen comb. As with the Light Infantry, the helmet lacked a front plate and the 'FII' cypher was merely painted on. The coat appears to have had thinner turn-backs and the powder horn was fixed to a green cord which was suspended from a padded green strap on the left shoulder. When not in use, the powder-horn was tucked into the right rear coat pocket. The right shoulder had one single standard shoulder-strap. Jagers had black leather cross-belts; one for the cartridge case and another for the bayonet scabbard and short sword; knapsack belts were also black. Unlike the regular infantry, they wore short boots, not gaiters. An unusual feature of the Jagers was that they are always depicted clean shaven with hair left untied (without a military queue) – a detail that sets them apart from all other troops. The principal armament was the 1769 Jager Stutzen, an excellent weapon; 1m long (with a 60 cm socket-bayonet) with a range of 300m in good conditions; this range was still over twice the range of a standard musket. Like all rifles, it had both advantages and disadvantages when compared to a musket; above all, it took training and skill to load and maintain, and it had a lower rate of fire.

Although both the Jagers and the Light Infantry were considered to be effective elite units, their small numbers reflected the low emphasis placed on light infantry throughout the Austrian army.

Figure 15: Pioneer Corporal: 'Hardegg' Pioneer Company: Main Column

There were seven specialist Pioneer companies at Marengo, of which four were attached to the Main Column's assault on Marengo. Each company was supposed to number approximately 100 men, though strengths must have varied considerably. It was the Pioneers who were tasked with bridging obstacles, including ravines and canals, and for ensuring clear routes of passage for the army.

Despite their presence, the Army seems to have struggled with poor terrain and obstacles throughout the battle. In particular, Pioneer officers at the battle showed poor forward planning. At the very start of the day, the Pioneers had failed to create a second opening in the fortified bridgehead at the Bormida. This delayed the deployment of troops and it took the Austrians some four hours to negotiate the bottleneck. Furthermore, despite knowing that they would have to cross the Fontanone, none of the Pioneer officers had been able to locate the portable Laufbrucken bridging equipment needed to cross. Major Hardegg eventually ordered his Pioneers into the Fontanone in human chains of 17 men. Up to their necks in water, these men supported a makeshift bridge of planks across a 7 metre-wide stretch of canal, until the arrival of the bridging equipment. At the same time, under the cover of artillery fire, they also widened the stone bridge on the main Tortona road.

It was these actions, performed under fire, that allowed the 63rd fusiliers and Lattermann's grenadiers to form bridgeheads across the Fontanone to the north of Marengo and directly in front of Marengo by the early afternoon. This was a key turning point in the battle. Once the Grenadiers had enough men across the Fontanone, they were able to mount a series of four assaults on the courtyard of Marengo itself; the last of which captured it.

72 The Austrian Imperial Army

Figure 16

Figure 15

The Pioneers had to work with the battle raging all around them, under heavy fire. Thanks to their perseverance, they managed to construct a footbridge. As soon as it was completed, General Lattermann ordered his grenadiers across and the courtyard of Marengo was stormed. The enemy counterattacked and succeeded in recapturing the courtyard temporarily, but the grenadiers held on to their positions beyond the ditch. Now the Pioneers were able to widen the walkway and also widen the passage over the stone bridge (on the road); this allowed our imperial troops to advance yet again.
Brinner

Later in the day, the Pioneers also appear to have been involved in the rear-guard fighting at Marengo as they attempted both to defend their two bridges and maintain them amidst the rush of retreating heavy cavalry and artillery.

Since all lines of retreat led to Marengo, a vast crowd of fleeing troops gravitated towards the crossing points. The beams of timber that formed these crossings over the Fontanone were only saved from collapse thanks to the work of the Pioneers. By 10 o'clock Marengo was once more attacked and captured by the enemy.
Brinner

Pioneer casualties appear to have been comparatively light, with even Hardegg's company losing only 4 dead and 10 captured; there is no mention of wounded. During this confused fighting around the bridging points in fading light, Pioneer-Corporal Seemann was mentioned in dispatches for bravery:

During the final French charge, Major Hardegg's company was in danger of being completely captured. Corporal Seemann was noted for an act of exceptional bravery. According to the wording of the Commission Report, enemy dragoons had over-run the company capturing a number of prisoners. Corporal Seemann collected a number of men and launched a determined counterattack which succeeded in freeing the prisoners, pushing back the dragoons and enabling the company to retreat safely. The Medal Commission duly awarded him the Silver Medal for his bravery on 14th August 1800.

This Pioneer corporal in Figure 15 carries a short 120cm dragoon carbine, a weapon often made from old reconditioned muskets. The rest of his uniform is an adapted version of the old pre-1798 infantry coat, as Pioneers were not issued with new pattern coats until well after 1800. Support troops were low on the priority list for new equipment. Although modified with a standing collar, the coat retains the distinctive turnbacks of the old pre-1798 coat and his sabre is still carried on an old-issue waist-belt. Facings were green and all pioneers wore the artillery-style round hat. His status as a Corporal is marked by his short sabre, though he has removed his other NCO distinctions; in full uniform, these would include a plume (all yellow with black tip), silver hat galloon-ribbon and a yellow-black-striped sword knot. Privates did not carry a sabre, and would have worn a black over yellow plume on parade. Officers wore an entirely black plume.

Despite the presence of pioneers, what the Austrians needed above all were their pontoneer companies. Large rivers like the Bormida could only be crossed using the pontoon bridge equipment handled by this specialist engineer corps. These men and their equipment had been sent over 30 km away by general Zach in an effort to mislead Bonaparte. Yet his limited battlefield experience led Zach to overlook the fact that he would need to bridge the Bormida opposite Castel Ceriolo as well as at the bridgehead. This was yet another oversight that contributed to the Austrian defeat.

Figure 16: Irregular Serezaner Scout: Attached to Banater Grenzer regiment: Fieldmarshal-Lieutenant O'Reilly's Third Column

The Third Column under Fieldmarshal-Lieutenant O'Reilly was assigned the southern flank of the Austrian Army. It was composed of regiments of irregular border infantry called Grenzers (see Fig. 17 and 18 below). However, each battalion of Grenzers also had a section of Balkan scouts, referred to as Heyducker or Serezaner. These were men recruited from the very fringes of the Ottoman controlled Balkans. They were often from the same areas where the Ottomans recruited their own Balkan light cavalry, called Spahis or sometimes Sipahis. In the mountainous terrain of northern Italy, they were used as scouts and guards. On campaign, they operated as mixed bands of mounted horsemen and foot soldiers, fighting for pay, muskets and booty. In the early 1790s, the Austrian Command paid them for each severed enemy head.

"In battle, they swarmed ahead of the regular regiments and engaged in skirmish fighting. They were often used for minor operations which required agility or daring or as guards for artillery depots or transport."
Ottenfeld

They wore their own ethnic clothing; their sole military equipment being an army issued red cloak, sometimes attached to a cape which acted as a hood. Figure 16 is based on two prints by Rugendas and Seele and contemporary prints of

Ottoman Arnaut (Albanian) levees. These sources show many of them wearing either a red felt cap or a black-felt fez. The split-toe boots are a detail from Ottenfeld.

The Serezaner scout in Figure 16 also carries a version of the 1772 Crespi breech-loading carbine. This innovative 122cm-long weapon had originally been designed for Austrian dragoons; it was one of the first carbines where the bullet, wad and powder could be loaded through a breech-clip above the trigger. However, problems with hot gas escaping from the breech caused the carbine to be withdrawn from service in the 1790s and thereafter allocated to the Grenzer battalions. The carbine also had an 80cm spear bayonet that fitted under the wooden stock when not in use.

Figure 17: Corporal: 1st Battalion 3rd Ogulin Grenzer Regiment: Fieldmarshal-Lieutenant O'Reilly's Third Column

The Grenzers were the irregular frontier militia of the Austrian Empire. They were recruited from settlers bordering the Ottoman Empire. In return for land, they owed military service to their regional militia. Militia regiments were drawn from various ethnic groups, depending on the border area in which the barracks and depots were based. However, the majority of the Grenzer regiments were Croat, and this was true of three of the four battalions present at Marengo. The Banat district battalion was the exception, having a significant intake of German-speaking Swabian border settlers. Unsuited to the rigid discipline and training imposed on regular regiments, Grenzer regiments were used as light-infantry troops, fighting in open order.

Marksmanship was a Grenzer speciality. Ottenfeld says that the Grenz regiments did not have Grenadiers, but had elite companies of 'sharpshooters' instead, numbering about 250 men per regiment. These companies usually formed the elite core of the Grenzer battalions sent on campaign to Italy. NCOs were also often trained as marksmen.

The 600 men of the 3rd Ogulin Regiment were mainly Croats and Slovenes from the Ogulin district. Together with the three other Grenzer battalions in Third Column, they spent the morning of the battle assaulting and capturing fixed French positions; first at Pietrabuona Farm and then the positions either side of La Stortigliona Farm to the South of Marengo. However, it was the Oguliners who led the assaults on La Stortigliona and Cascina Bianca, supported by the 8th Nauendorff Hussars. Stutterheim describes their part in the battle:

'It was a fine clear day with a cool westerly breeze moderating the heat of the sun. The first column to file across the bridge was that commanded by Fieldmarshal-Lieutenant O'Reilly. This vanguard had no more than 2,228 infantry and some 769 cavalry. They attacked the French outposts driving them out of the buildings and barns of Pietrabona. After this attack, they moved to the right along the road that leads to Spinetta and Frugarolo, thereby giving way to the main column following from behind ...
Earl O'Reilly was deceived by the small group of skirmishers at la Stortigliona farm. His attack on La Stortigliona drew him too far to the right causing him to lose contact with the main body of the army. O'Reilly continued to advance towards the right (the south), coming upon an enemy battalion that had deployed at Ca' Bianca, an hour from Frugarolo. This was attacked by the Ogulin battalion, whilst our cavalry surrounded it, causing it to surrender.
Stutterheim

The sharpshooter in Figure 17 is from the elite sharpshooter company of the Regiment. He wears the white uniform usually supplied to Grenz regiments on campaign, with the orange facings of the 3rd Oguliners. His uniform would have been a pre-1798 infantry coat, complete with turnbacks, falling collar, waistbelt and infantry sabre. The uniform and equipment of Grenz sharpshooters is well documented. The Artaria prints (1793-9), the 1799 Zurich manuscript, together with prints in the Vienna War Museum and the Vinkhuijzen collection all show similar uniforms with minor variations. All show the klobuck felt hat in its various forms; they also show blue Hungarian trousers and boots. *

This sharpshooter carries a version of the 1779 pattern Girardoni Air Rifle and its equipment bag. Grenzers are shown using this rifle throughout this period. A superb weapon if properly used, it fired bullets preloaded in a 22-bullet magazine-tube which was also breech-loaded. The fire-power came from a screw-on air-chamber (in the rifle butt). It could fire 22 shots in fairly rapid succession, without flash. The bag carried a spare pre-pumped air-chamber and spare pre-loaded tubes, as well as a hand pump for use in the field. Each sharpshooter company also had a large air-pressure machine to fill the chambers prior to battle. Girardoni sharpshooters are shown carrying a pike with a metal hook, on which they could aim the rifle. Although lacking the muzzle velocity of a standard rifle, it was still a deadly, accurate weapon over shorter ranges, able to fire multiple times.

Ottenfeld says that repeated attempts to introduce white Hungarian style trousers to some Grenz regiments were unpopular and met with varying success. The majority may still have worn blue.

77 The Austrian Imperial Army

Figure 17

78   The Austrian Imperial Army

Figure 18

Figure 18: NCO Sharpshooter: 1st Battalion, 5th Warasdin-Kreutz Regiment: Fieldmarshal-Lieutenant O'Reilly's Third Column

The 5th Warasdin-Kreutz had already fought the French around Marengo the day before the battle, losing over 100 casualties. The French 24th Legere and 44th demi-brigades had attacked and captured Marengo, driving out the Grenzers stationed there. The attack had taken the outnumbered Austrians by surprise. Stutterheim was able to observe the closing stages of this fire-fight.

The day before the battle, without any warning, at about 6 o'clock the artillery on the city walls suddenly opened up with everything they had. No-one knew what was happening but everyone hurried to their horses. When we got to the town gate, we could see a multitude of French skirmishers running along the opposite bank of the Bormida. The bridge-head guns were blasting away in full barrage. Bullets were whistling through the camp and everyone was in motion, rushing to arms. It transpired that these were the advance troops of General Gardanne, who had just over-run General O'Reilly's outposts. The officers present ordered the Splenyi regiment, encamped near the bridge, to form up and make a sortie out of the bridgehead. This sortie was supported by the artillery that had been brought up in front of the camp and was successful in pushing the enemy away from the bridgehead, which was now no longer in range of their artillery. This allowed our army to continue to use the bridge and bridgehead, but the Fontanone ditch and the area around the courtyard of Marengo had been lost; furthermore, this was the very point from which we hoped to launch our planned attack on the following day.
Stutterheim

Grenzer uniforms had changed little since the mid-1790s. Ottenfeld says that Grenzer regiments were directed not to re-equip with new uniforms and equipment during the 1798-1800 period. These orders set out a transition period for different parts of the army to adopt the new 1798 uniform. Light infantry units would be the first to re-equip followed by Line regiments. In contrast, Grenzers and garrison troops were to be supplied with stocks of old-pattern uniforms until these had fully run out, although these might be reconditioned or altered where possible.

In 1800, Grenzers continued to wear two distinct uniforms, often side by side. The first was the brown militia coat, worn on border duty; the second was based on the white infantry coat of standard line regiments, often supplied just before the start of a campaign. The Grenzer in Figure 18 is based on different prints by Seele, Rugendas, Bleuler and other prints in the Vienna War Archives for the period 1797-1800. Although all these prints show variations in the uniform, there were common traits. These included: Hungarian infantry trousers and boots; a brown coat, often with braiding; and a sabre or sword carried on a waist-belt. Based on a print by Rugendas, this Grenzer wears a felt 'klobuck' hat with a detachable peak; the black and yellow plume and yellow upper band mark him out as an NCO. The klobuck felt hat could take various forms and dimensions (see Fig. 17 above) and was more often worn without a peak; later versions were shaped like shakos. A greatcoat or cloak is often shown draped over the top and sides of the knapsack.

Grenzers were armed with a variety of muskets, but select NCOs and Sharpshooter companies were given rifles; usually old-pattern rifles no longer used by the more elite Jagers. One of these outdated models was the Austrian 1768-pattern double-barrel 'Doppelstutzen fur Grenzer' (105cm long). This was still a very effective weapon and French tirailleurs would capture and re-use them when they could.* Only the upper barrel was rifled; the lower was smoothbore.

Despite their skills as frontiers marksmen, the Grenzers were treated with diffidence by the Austrian High Command. The extended campaigns throughout 1799-1800 had left the Grenzers poorly supplied and unhappy at their enforced absence from home. There had been mutinies in some Grenzer units in Italy prior to Marengo and (rightly or wrongly) O'Reilly's Column was seen as the weakest element in the army.

Grenzer Uniforms at Marengo

2nd Ottocac Regiment 1st Battalion	Yellow facings, white buttons
3rd Ogulin Regiment 1st Battalion	Orange facings, yellow buttons
5th Warasdin -Kreutz Regiment 1st Battalion	Crab red facings, yellow buttons
4th Banat District Grenz Battalion	Crimson facings, yellow buttons

The memoire of a Russian prisoner describes French light infantry using these very same double-barrelled rifles.

Figure 19: Oberleutnant: 1st Battalion, 23rd Regiment 'Toscana': Main Column: Initial attacks on Marengo.
Figure 20: Senior Staff Officer: Staff of Fieldmarshal-Lieutenant Ott: Second Column: Northern Flank of the battlefield.

Each regimental company, at full complement, was led by a Captain, an Oberleutnant, an Unterleutnant, an Ensign, a Sergeant-Major and a Quartermaster as well as 13 other non-commissioned officers; in addition to this, there were officer cadets and other support officers attached to regimental headquarters. These infantry officers were the men who made the Austrian military system work, yet contemporaries were concerned by the state of the infantry officer corps. For one thing, officers' pay had remained unchanged since the 1750s and becoming an army officer was widely seen as a career of last resort. By 1800, the increasingly low level of education of infantry officer recruits forced the military Colleges to teach basic addition, subtraction and multiplication; a low-level education unthinkable in the artillery.

Commissioned Austrian company officers all wore the same uniform, without official distinction between ranks. Although full dress was a long-tailed white coat, company officers are nearly always depicted wearing a light-grey 'undress' version of this coat. Kininger Vicenz, Lejeune and Rugendas all show Austrian Junior Officers wearing these coats. There are no contemporary prints before 1805 showing officers wearing the dark grey Oberrock greatcoat. Furthermore, company officers continued to wear the bicorn on campaign throughout 1799-1800, without exception. They wore an epee sword (sabres for Hungarian officers) on a white belt and sling; this was covered by a yellow sash with black stripes, knotted on the left. A pistol holster was worn on a cross-belt passing over the right shoulder, sometimes held in place by a single right-shoulder strap. Company officers were expected to lead from the front, as the experience of Captain Josef Rauch of the 23rd Regiment 'Toscana' shows:

'As the regiment advanced (towards the Fontanone ditch) it had already begun to pass through cultivated terrain. This was arable land broken up by ditches, meadows and bushes with the field of view limited in all directions. This gave cover to the enemy facing us and acted as a barrier so that our cavalry could not support us at all. Ignoring these obstacles, we mounted a determined assault.

82 The Austrian Imperial Army

Figure 19

Figure 20

However, the musket fire was so ferocious that I had never experienced anything like that before…I came through unwounded but my coat and equipment were shot through with bullet holes.'
Rauch

The dress of Senior Officers differed to that of company officers, reflecting the wide social gulfs between junior and senior ranks. Whilst many Junior Officers came from the provincial gentry, the senior ranks were the preserve of the aristocracy or those who had married in to this exclusive elite. It is true that talented officers of non-aristocratic parentage like Zach or O'Reilly could sometimes rise to prominence, but they remained on the periphery – often subject to social disdain. The deeply conservative nature of the Austrian officer class was a contributory factor in the factional divisions which weakened the Austrian Command in 1800. Stutterheim describes a system where there was a lack of professional competence in the higher echelons of leadership. High-born Generals and Senior Officers often had little effective battle-field experience and remained reliant on more professional subordinates.

'In charge of the administration of the High Command was Colonel Graf Radetzky, a man of restless activity, witty and enterprising. Other Senior Generals, with the exception of Hadik and Vukassovich, were of little consequence, lacking in initiative and talent. Generals like Kahn, Ott, Schellenberg, Gottesheim and others, were not fit to lead a regiment let alone a brigade; all had to be left to the direction of the officers assigned to them by the Quartermaster General's staff and merely gave their names to important orders or dispositions.'
Stutterheim

Younger officers like Niepperg and Crossard bemoaned the fact that Generals** tended to stick to written orders, showing little or no initiative.

'At Marengo, the French army was allowed to continue its retreat, without our own right and left corps making an effort to attack them on either the flanks or rear. Despite facing comparatively weak opposition, these two corps did not think of changing their plan of action. They (Generals Ott and O'Reilly) had no new orders so they simply took no initiative. These same men strictly adhered to their written orders, to the great disadvantage of the army. This does not reflect favourably on their professional competency.'
Niepperg

Apart from Staff Officers and Generals, Senior ranks in each regiment included the regimental Commanding Officer (the Inhaber), the Lieutenant Colonel and two regimental Majors. The Senior Officer in Figure 20 wears a typical uniform shown in pictorial sources from 1799-1800, including Lejeune, Rovatti and Rugendas. The 1798 regulations prescribed an officer's coat with a simple standing collar; however, this is never shown for this period. Officers continued to wear older red stand-and-fall collars with red cuffs. For Generals and above, the red collars and cuffs were edged with a distinctive criss-cross gold galloon ribbon (see inset), which varied according to rank; generals also wore red cloth breeches for full-dress and sometimes red turn-backs and lining to their coats. Generals are also shown wearing high (above the knee) riding boots. Epee belts were gold thread with two horizontal black borders with brass and silver imperial eagle buckles. The officers' sash was silk. Senior officers' bicorns were also edged in galloon ribbon with a green ribbon-cockade and plume.

Additionally, administrative adjutant officers wore a green version of the officers' coat.

*The crescent standard featured inset is one of the more unusual objects depicted being carried into battle in a 1799 print of the battle of Verona. Possibly a captured Turkish standard.
**Although Austrian Generals had different titles of rank, including Fieldmarshal Lieutenant or General-Major, Austrian army commentators and contemporaries like Niepperg and Stutterheim continued to refer to them as Generals – the author has done the same.

The Austrian Cavalry

The Austrian Imperial cavalry had been reputedly the best in Europe. Moreover, the Austrian High Command had hoped its overwhelming numerical advantage in cavalry would gain them victory at Marengo. They were a strong force fielding over 9 regiments with a total of 7,500 troops. Yet mainly composed of dragoons and hussars, they lacked a complement of heavy cavalry. This would be significant in the battle. Moreover, the way cavalry was used in the battle may well have compounded this weakness. Witnesses to the battle, like Crossard, note that the cavalry was split up and wasted on poorly conceived attacks:

'The regiments of the 9th Lichtenstein Dragoons and of the 10th Lobkowitz Light-Horse covered our area on the northern flank of the army. The 10th Lobkowitz in particular, was one of the most distinguished cavalry regiments but had the misfortune to lose their commanding Colonel, the excellent Marquis de Sommariva, who had been transferred. The rest of our cavalry was scattered to the south of the battlefield. General Orelli, one of the senior cavalry

commanders, rode up to me saying: 'You were right! They want us to be destroyed piecemeal!"
Crossard

The collapse and flight of a large part of the Austrian cavalry at the end of the battle was the main reason for the Austrian defeat. It can perhaps be explained by the fact that almost every cavalry squadron had been heavily committed throughout the day. Napoleonic cavalry was a weapon that could only be used sparingly; after multiple charges, the horses could become 'blown' or exhausted. Since it was the power and momentum of the horse that gave cavalry its advantage, this would eventually render it ineffective for the remainder of the battle. Niepperg was even more scathing;

'When by late afternoon, Our High Command wanted to order the cavalry to pursue the defeated enemy and deal the final blow, there was widespread consternation. No one knew where the cavalry was! The good judgement of our commanders had so consumed it, dispersed it and detached it, that it was now scattered throughout the battlefield; broken up into squadrons, half-squadrons and even platoons. Furthermore, the 1st Kaiser and 4th Karaczay Dragoons had lost so many men in the passage of the ditch at Marengo that our victorious army now found itself without cavalry. On this vast plain, we had no choice but to use a swarm of skirmishers and volunteer infantry to pursue the French rearguard in open terrain. The French rearguard was chiefly composed of cavalry, superbly led by general Kellermann, who constantly threatened these skirmishers, who themselves remained without cavalry support. The few remaining horsemen we had, advanced in a state of lowest morale, upset by the pointless losses suffered earlier in the day.'
Niepperg

It is true that by the end of the day, the horses and men of the surviving squadrons would have been exhausted. Whatever the reason, it was the supporting cavalry screen of Austrian dragoons that broke and fled during Desaix's counterattack, starting a general rout.

Dragoon Uniforms at Marengo

General Pilatti's Dragoon Brigade
1st Kaiser Dragoons	Poppy Red facings, yellow buttons
4th Karaczay Dragoons	Poppy Red facings, white buttons

General Nobili's Dragoon Brigade
3rd Erzherzog Johann Dragoons	Orange facings, yellow buttons
9th Lichtenstein Dragoons	Black facings, white buttons

O'Reilly's Third Column
8th Wurtemberg Dragoons	Grey facings, yellow buttons

Ott's Second Column
10th Lobkowitz Dragoons	Light Blue facings, white buttons

86 The Austrian Imperial Army

Figure 21

Figure 22

87 The Austrian Imperial Army

Figure 23

Figure 21: Trooper: 10th 'Lobkowitz' Dragoons: Second Column: Fieldmarshal-Lieutenant Ott: Advance on Castel Ceriolo in the northern part of the battlefield.

Figure 22: Rittmeister (Captain): 3rd 'Erzherzog Johann' Dragoons: Main Column: Initial advance on Marengo.

The 3rd Erzherzog Johann Dragoons were brigaded with the 9th Lichtenstein Dragoons under the command of General-Major Nobili. They were just two of six dragoon regiments at the battle; four of these being concentrated in the Main Column's attack on Marengo. These were very large regiments, numbering between 750 and 1050 cavalry; as large as an entire French cavalry brigade of three regiments.

The 3rd Erzherzog Johann were meant to be the reserve force, held back, ready to pursue the defeated French army. In the event, they found themselves heavily committed throughout the day. In particular, once the Austrian infantry had captured Marengo, it was the dragoons who initially charged the squares of French infantry retreating along the road. Stutterheim describes the situation he saw:

'After this defeat of the Consular Guard, all resistance on the part of the French ceased. Only their cavalry tried to offer some resistance on a few occasions, but even they retreated every time our own cavalry advanced. However, our cavalry had begun to disperse, so that we could take little advantage of the costly victory won by our infantry. Meanwhile, we had captured 10 guns, 2 howitzers, several ammunition carts and about 3000 prisoners. The battlefield was littered with dead and wounded, and I had never seen the French army in such a state of disarray. Their infantry were in full rout and completely dispersed, fleeing across this vast plain towards San Giuliano. If, at that time, we had an enterprising general to lead our cavalry, I am certain that not even a tenth of the French army would have escaped. Never was a more perfect victory won. But fate was to decree that not only would this victory be of little use to us, it would in fact bring us disaster.'
Stutterheim

By the time of the final Austrian pursuit at about 5pm, Austrian cavalry were in very poor morale and riding blown tired-out horses. Once the French counterattack commenced, they would also not have been able to judge the strength of the counterattacking force. Nevertheless, the flight of the Austrian cavalry was the single most important cause of the unexpected collapse of the Austrian army:

I was very upset to witness the retreat of the 9th Lichtenstein Dragoons from my vantage point on the outskirts of Castel Ceriolo. The 10th Lobkowitz Light-Horse also rode through the area, led by Prince de Latour Taxis. I expressed by astonishment to the Prince, at this sudden turn of events. However, my low rank meant I could do nothing to remedy the situation, whatever I thought. Moreover, my horse was by now overwhelmed with fatigue. I could do nothing.
Crossard

The blame for the flight was laid formally on the 9th Lichtenstein Dragoons, who were disbanded after the battle. The 3rd Erzherzog Johann would survive to take part in the battle of Austerlitz 5 years later, reformed as the 1st Erzherzog Johann Heavy Dragoons. Stutterheim describes the reaction of the Lichtenstein Dragoons to the French counterattack:

'*The leaders of those regiments of dragoons (the 9th Lichtenstein and 3rd Erzherzog) were unable to form up their troops or to bring aid to our infantry who were being surrounded. While our cavalry were still forming up, they were attacked and put to flight by Kellermann's brigade, a much weaker force. General Zach later claimed that the Lichtenstein Dragoon Regiment immediately turned around and retreated, as soon as it saw the French cavalry; in doing this, it caused the flight of the other regiment. Zach claimed that the French cavalry hesitated at first and did not seem to want to charge at our cavalry, which was superior to them. For this act, the Lichtenstein regiment was later reduced. The French counterattack had such a damaging effect precisely because it was so surprising and so unexpected. The flight of this cavalry was followed by that of all the different army units which had hitherto pursued the enemy. Everything returned towards Marengo in the same disorder as everything had advanced towards San Giuliano. The hundreds of wagons lining the road to Alessandria, carrying Austrian and enemy wounded increased the confusion. The screams of fleeing soldiers spread a sense of panic and terror which gripped the entire army. Yet we were only being pursued by a few hundred horsemen.*'
Stutterheim

Dragoons were meant to be general all-purpose troops, able to carry out both the role of light and heavy cavalry. However, most Austrian dragoons rode smaller, light horses and used a raised light cavalry saddle to give them extra height. Like the 10th Lobkowitz, many of these regiments had been originally formed as Chevaulegers or Light-Horse and would later be redesignated as Chevaulegers after 1801. Their French dragoon counterparts rode much larger horses; an advantage that would prove to be critical in the battle.

Their uniform was based on a green cavalry coat; it had wide split tails, ten metal buttons and a single shoulder strap on the left shoulder. Regimental facings were worn on the collar, cuffs, shoulder strap and edge of the turn-backs. The standing collar was usually short, exposing the black neck-stock. Breeches were of white cloth and boots were the same as those worn by the Hussars, though buttoned riding trousers were worn on campaign. All dragoons wore the new leather cavalry helmet, very similar to that being introduced to the infantry. The brass front plate bore an FII imperial cypher. NCO distinctions included gloves, an NCO cane and a gilded finish to the helmet front plate. Only NCOs and officers wore riding gloves.

Dragoons were armed with a straight bladed dragoon sword with an 84cm blade and simple steel stirrup hilt (see inset). The guard on some sword hilts could open out to form a double-guard as in Figure 21; the scabbard was steel. The sword was suspended from a white waist-belt with slings. When on foot, the slings could be hitched up to the belt, suspending the scabbard higher off the ground. A loop in the belt could also be used for carrying a pistol.

Most dragoons also carried the Austrian 1798 standard dragoon carbine, which was just over 120cm long, fixed in a sling on the right side of the saddle harness. A small number of sharp-shooters in each squadron may have been armed with the short-muzzled 1780 cavalry rifle. They also carried a carbine-clip cross-belt over the same left shoulder as the cartridge-pouch belt; these are shown fixed together with a metal stud. A thin grey strap for the canteen was worn on the right shoulder.

Cavalry Rittmeisters, like the officer in Figure 22, carried a rank equivalent to that of Captain and commanded one of the 6 squadrons in a regiment. At Marengo each squadron would have had between 140-180 men, on average. Distinctions for cavalry officers included a finer cut and quality of uniform. This was most visible in the helmet which included a gilded front plate and a brass crest for the black over yellow woollen comb. The upper edges of the cuffs and collar were also finished with gold galloon ribbon. The officer in Figure 22 wears a yellow comb with black transverse stripes, shown in two figures by Lejeune of 3rd Dragoon officers. This is unusual but is the only depiction of 3rd Dragoon officers and was painted by an eyewitness present at the battle; a highly reliable eyewitness. Other distinctions included a silk or camel hair sash (depending on seniority); again, Lejeune shows this as yellow with transverse black stripes. The sword scabbard was leather with three steel bands and had a yellow and black sword knot. Officer's saddle cloths were also finished in gold thread as shown in the inset image.

The 10th Lobkowitz Dragoons had already suffered significant losses at the battle of Casteggio-Montebello on the 9th June. Four days later, at Marengo they were covering the flanks of Ott's Second Column. As the afternoon progressed they were drawn into a series of counter-charges to prevent a succession of French regiments advancing on Castel Ceriolo, including the advance of the Consular Guard. Although limited in success, these counter-charges helped to secure Austrian control of this northern flank. The 10th Lobkowitz would also play a central role at Austerlitz in 1805, renamed and reformed as the 3rd O'Reilly Chevauleger.

Figure 23: Trooper: 4th 'Karaczay' Dragoons: Main Column: Initial advance on Marengo.

The 4th Karaczay Dragoons were brigaded with the 1st Kaiser Dragoons, under General-Major Pilatti. Both regiments had poppy-red facings, with only the button colour being different; the Kaiser had yellow and the Karaczay had white buttons. However, the Karaczay regiment formed the larger element of the brigade with over a thousand horse. Early on in the battle, they were ordered, under protest, to attempt a crossing of the Fontanone to the south of Marengo. Without support, the cavalrymen who crossed to the opposite bank were counter-attacked by French heavy cavalry – the survivors being shot off their horses by French infantry. Furthermore, the remaining squadrons were later committed to charges against French infantry columns retreating from Marengo. By late afternoon, this brigade ceased to be an effective force. Melas' order to cross the Fontanone by a narrow ford appears to have been particularly ill-conceived:

This order to cross the Fontanone was carried out with great difficulty and under duress. Very slowly, the troopers crossed one by one. These two regiments had scarcely begun to form up on the other side of the ditch, when they were spotted by General Kellermann who immediately attacked with two regiments of cavalry. The men who crossed were thrown back into the ditch. Many were killed in the crush to recross the ditch. Others towards the rear had to scatter through territory held by the enemy, hoping to cut their way through. Most were killed or captured, whilst others were only able to return after several days. This disaster severely damaged the morale of the remainder of our cavalry.
Stutterheim

Niepperg also emphasised how the incident effectively destroyed the brigade:

The brave Lieutenant-Colonel Baron de Kees of the regiment of the Kaiser's Light-Horse was wounded and taken prisoner beyond this ditch, which destroyed the morale of the troopers he commanded. These two regiments were unable to fight for the remainder of the battle. The enemy again occupied the opposite bank of the ditch, and could even have brought the attack to our side of the ditch, had they not been stopped by the grenadiers of General Weidenfeld.
Niepperg

Figure 23 shows the standard equipment and horse furniture of dragoon troopers. The saddle, bridle and horse furniture were those used by all Austrian light cavalry in the period. The rolled greatcoat and blanket were placed at the front of the saddle, giving added protection to the rider. The saddle cloth was red with a yellow border and two black stripes; a black sheepskin covered both the saddle cloth and the red valise fixed behind the cavalrymen. The carbine was carried in a sling on the right of the saddle, tied to a tent pole. A black leather pouch and white forage sack were also carried on this side of the saddle, to the rear of the rider. The left side of the saddle was kept free for the dragoon's sword.

Figure 24: Jager zu Pferd: Bussy Horse Jager: Advance Guard: Initial advance on Marengo and attack on Consular Guard.

'Our vanguard was commanded by Colonel de Frimont of the Chasseurs de Bussy. The enemy outposts allowed us to approach to within a hundred paces and after firing a few volleys, retreated behind the ditch, where the French had their main position. These were the same Chasseurs de Bussy who later covered themselves in glory by destroying the greater part of the Grenadiers of the Consular Guard, capturing 4 guns.'
Niepperg

The Austrian Horse Jager were considered elite light cavalry. Although there were only two small squadrons at Marengo probably numbering 186 men, they had an effect far beyond their small numbers. Part of the reason for this may be that they included a high number of French émigré cavalry in their ranks.

French memoires appear to see them everywhere in the course of the battle. Many of these memoires may simply be confusing them with Austrian dragoons. Nevertheless, their role as forward scouts would have placed them in the front line

93 The Austrian Imperial Army

Figure 24

of advancing Austrian cavalry, and this would have made them highly visible. They certainly took an active role in spearheading the attack which destroyed the Consular Guard, against whom they would have harboured a particularly bitter resentment.

The main role of the Bussy Horse Jager was in forward scouting and this also frequently brought them in contact with the French. Petit mentions the capture of a Bussy officer prior to the battle:

A group of prisoners and deserters were brought in to us. Amongst them was an officer of the Bussy Legion who wore the cross of St Lewis. The Consul questioned them at length on many details. When they were told that the person who had just spoken to them was none other than Bonaparte, they were speechless.
Petit

There were a considerable number of French émigré officers in Austrian service. Many thousands of French officers had fled during the early revolution, finding alternative commissions in foreign armies. Many sought service in French speaking units like the Bussy Horse Jagers. Not all of these men were motivated by political enmity. As the memoires of the émigré cavalryman Francois de Cezac shows, their attitude to fighting their fellow countrymen was ambivalent;

In this attack, we captured a number of French prisoners who were very helpful in carrying away our wounded. The prisoners were relieved to see there were no reprisals taken against them and that they were being treated as brothers and fellow countrymen. We requisitioned all the carts we could for the transport of the wounded. It was from that period that French Republicans and French Royalists began to see each other in a better light and this slowly helped to lessen political tensions.
de Cezac

The Horse Jager uniform followed the cut of the standard dragoon coat (see inset), although dyed grey with green facings. Cross-belts were black, as was the waistbelt, which was buckled on the right side. The helmet was similar to that worn by Jager infantry and horse furniture was identical to that used by the dragoons, as was the sword. They were armed with the short muzzled 69cm long 1789 cavalry rifle, with the rifle ramrod attached to their cartridge pouch strap. Horse Jagers appear in many contemporary prints and pictures, including the Mollo prints and works by Bradford, Kobell and Kininger Vicenz. It was a

Bussy officer who brought the very unwelcomed news of the French capitulation at Genoa:

We had stopped by some vineyards lining the side of the road when a Bussy Chasseur was brought in to General Lannes. This man said he was a deserter and presented Lannes with a printed copy of Massena's recent capitulation at Genoa. He told us that the entire Austrian army was now ranged against us. This individual was obviously sent by the Austrian High Command, but it transpired that his bad news was indeed true.
Nogues

Figure 25: Trooper: 7th Hussars: General Major Nimbsch's Brigade: Detached early in battle to the south of Alessandria.

The Austrians had a powerful force of elite Hussar regiments at Alessandria. Perhaps the strongest unit was GM Nimbsch's Brigade of 2,300 cavalry; it comprised the 7th Hussars and the 9th Erdody Hussars, both battle-hardened units. However, in the early stages of the battle as the French were frantically marshalling every available unit, the Austrian High Command sent this brigade away from the battlefield.

Melas and Zach had received reports of a force of French cavalry advancing from the south-east and believed this could be a strong advance force sent by the French Army of Italy. So confident was Zach of his superiority in cavalry and artillery that he sent the entire Hussar brigade to intercept this imagined threat. This one single decision may have lost him the battle. Yet this was not the only cavalry unit sent away from the main army. Another regiment, the 2nd Erzherzog Joseph Regiment of 1,100 men was sent 25 miles north-east towards Casale, the day before the battle

If these 3,400 Hussars had been present at the closing stages of the battle, there would have been no Austrian rout. At most, the French counter-attack would have blocked the Austrian advance towards San Giuliano. However, poor decisions were not the preserve of the Austrian High Command; they permeated the higher echelons of leadership at all levels. In the ensuing hours, General Nimbsch also lacked the presence of mind to return to the battle with at least part of his powerful force of cavalry.

On the morning of the battle, Melas and Zach ordered Nimbsch's entire hussar brigade back over the Bormida bridges towards Alessandria, where they then rode south several miles towards the imagined threat. What they encountered was a

96   The Austrian Imperial Army

Figure 25

small force of French dragoons and the 12th Chasseurs stationed far to the south, on the opposite bank of the Bormida.   The Brigade recrossed the Bormida for the third time that day and attacked and easily routed the 350 French chasseurs. Then, following orders to the letter, they appear to have returned towards Alessandria; but not towards the battle. Niepperg, who was an officer in the 7th Hussars, voices the bitterness and frustration that many officers felt at this:

'While the army was passing the Bormida in the morning, the report came that a few hundred French cavalry had attacked a squadron of Kaiser Dragoons stationed at Acqui and were already pursuing them along the banks of the Bormida and the Tanaro towards Alessandria. General Nimbsch, who with the 7th Hussar Regiment and 9th Erdödy Regiment, received an order signed by Melas from Lieutenant Hugelmann to go with his brigade towards the enemy cavalry and attack them. This brigade consisted of 2,341 hussars.
Major Fulda, who formed the vanguard of this brigade with two squadrons attacked the French cavalry without hesitation, chased them back as far as Acqui, and took most of them prisoner. From them, he learnt that the French main force (of the Army of Italy) was still far away in the mountains. The mission came to an end here with Fulda ensuring there would be no attack on Alessandria. However, beyond the Bormida, the battle raged. It did not occur to the Commander in Chief to summon this brigade, nor did it occur to their commander (Nimbsch) to hasten towards the battle.   These brave regiments of hussars merely dismounted on the road to Acqui, south of the city; unable to share the burden of their comrades.'
Niepperg

Hussars were an exclusively Hungarian branch of light cavalry in Austrian service.   The 7th Hussars were a prestigious unit, unusual in not being assigned the 'name' of an inhaber (Commander in Chief).   They had already taken part in several successful actions during the 1800 campaign, notably the capture of the Alpine pass at Mont Cenis.

There are several prints and paintings of the 7th Hussars by Kininger, Rugendas and other un-named artists – two of them showing the hussars in engagements during the 1799-1800 campaigns. The Hussar in Figure 25 is based on these sources. The light blue pelisse was worn as a jacket with the braiding attached to 3 columns of white buttons. The yellow and black braiding was arranged in standard horizontal rows or in the zig-zag style unique to Hungarian hussars.

A blue dolman jacket may have been worn under the pelisse, which also had about 15-16 rows of braid linked to three columns of white buttons.   Hussar buttons could be either white or yellow, depending on the regiment. The breeches had lace along their outer seams and a simple trefoil design at the top of each leg, sometimes called a Hungarian knot (see inset in Fig. 26)

The shako was 8 inches high and made of felt, reinforced with leather. Originally introduced in 1798, the newer patterns of shako had become slightly taller and wider at the top. A chin strap was fixed to the shako at two points, both behind and in front of the ear. The shako bore a brass version of the national cockade, a woollen pompom, a black over yellow plume and a circling row of braid attached to raquettes. Contemporary depictions for this regiment show these shakos being worn in a variety of ways: with or without peaks, and with and without plumes. One should note that the cockade was positioned very low down on the shako; a detail that is often overlooked in later 19th century drawings. Finally, the tall 36cm plume was often given even greater height on formal occasions by the addition of tall black feathers. Hussars were steeped in longstanding traditions; for example, they continued to wear their hair in plaited cadenettes, tied back to form a queue.

The standard Hussar sabretache would sometimes have been covered with a waterproof oil-skin on campaign. A second pattern of this post-1798 sabretache with more rounded edges is shown in the inset in Fig.26 below. The horse harness was a light cavalry harness; and the saddle was the raised Hungarian saddle. The saddle-cloth and associated equipment was similar to that of Austrian Dragoons, but the cut of the Hussar saddle-cloth ended in a pointed angle at the rear.

The standard 1769 pattern Austrian light cavalry sabre (with an 83cm blade) was now carried in a plain metal scabbard on slings suspended from a dark-red leather waist-belt. Older scabbards (black leather with two metal bands and metal chape) were still common. The sword knot was also of red leather, though brown is also shown by Kobell.

The inset image shows the new models of short carbine and pistol being introduced in this period. The short 86cm 'Karabiner fur Husaren' 1798 model, had a long metal bar on its left side so that it could be attached to the cross-belt clip. Select marksmen in each squadron would also have been armed with either the short cavalry rifle (see Horse Jager above) or the older 105cm long cavalry rifle. The fact that this strong cavalry division was sent away from the battlefield on the very morning of the battle amazed French observers as much as it angered more competent Austrian officers. General Victor found this decision difficult to comprehend:

'At this time, Melas had been informed that an Austrian squadron at Acqui had been obliged to retreat in the face of a much larger unit of French cavalry. He jumped to the conclusion that Suchet (of the Army of Italy) could not be far. All he had to do was a simple calculation of the distance and time, without even considering the powerful fortifications of Alessandria or the obstacle of the Bormida itself; all these factors should have allayed any fears. Instead, he judged it necessary to detach 17 entire squadrons, 2,340 cavalry, sending them to Cantalupo. In doing this he significantly weakened the very cavalry in which he placed his greatest hope of achieving victory.'
Victor

Figure 26: Corporal: 5th Hussars: Attached to O'Reilly's Third Column – also supporting advance on San Giuliano at closing stages of battle.

Figure 27: Rittmeister (Captain): 8th 'Nauendorff' Hussars: Attached to O'Reilly's Third Column – encircling charge against Consular Guard.

There was yet another Hussar brigade that was not sent away from the battlefield. This smaller unit of 530 cavalrymen, comprised two squadrons from the 5th Hussars and two squadrons from the 8th Nauendorff Hussars. This brigade supported the Grenzer infantry of O'Reilly's column throughout the morning. During the French withdrawal, squadrons from the 8th Nauendorff attacked the rear of the Consular Guard together with the Bussy Horse Jager, forcing their surrender.

Elements of the 5th hussars may also have participated in this charge. However, at least some squadrons of the 8th Hussars remained on the southern flank of the battle where they forced the surrender of French infantry at Cascina Bianca. The 5th Hussars also appear to have been present at the final stages of the battle, as Lejeune depicts two Hussars from the 5th – one surrendering, the other fleeing. Once operating on the open plain, these two small Hussar regiments had a significant impact on events. Crossard explains why they were so effective:

The advance from (Castel Ceriolo)took place on a vast plain. Here the cavalry and artillery could riddle the enemy with grapeshot before charging. The nature of the terrain enabled us to hold the enemy at a distance (under artillery fire) for

100 The Austrian Imperial Army

Figure 26

101 The Austrian Imperial Army

Figure 27

as long as we deemed fit, or until we decided to charge. The artillery of the enemy was also powerless against our cavalry, having been neutralised by the superior number of cannons we employed at Marengo.

The enemy artillery was rendered even more ineffective because our cavalry could manoeuvre to ensure that it always had the French infantry between it and the Marengo guns. The French artillery could not fire on us for fear of harming their own troops.

Crossard's frustration was that only a fraction of the Austrian cavalry was able to properly deploy on the plain. The colourful uniform of the 5th Hussars led to several contemporary depictions. One by Kininger Vicenz probably dates to 1807 (the year when short hair became mandatory) and two earlier prints in the Vinkhuizjen collection are marked as originating from the Vienna War Archives. Figure 26 is based on these sources. It shows an NCO in full campaign uniform, wearing campaign riding trousers. Austrian riding-trousers did not have leather reinforcement on the inner-leg, but were made from tough grey canvas. His NCO distinctions include the NCO cane, gloves and a double lace band on the shako though he carried the same steel-hilt sword as privates (only Sergeant-Majors and above had brass hilts). The uniform of the 9th Erdody Hussars (detached from the battlefield) was identical to that of the 5th, except that they wore a black shako.

Rittmeister was a rank equating to Captain in command of a squadron. The Rittmeister in Figure 27 wears full formal parade dress. Full uniform included coloured cloth breeches, dolman, plume and barrel sash – items that were sometimes also worn on the battlefield by officers and NCOs. In full parade-dress, the more practical pelisse was slung over the left shoulder and attached to a braided loop over the right shoulder. Cuffs and collars on Hungarian Hussar dolmans were always the same colour as the dolman itself. Significant distinctions for officers were metallic braiding and lace throughout the uniform. Officers' dolmans and pelisses usually had 5 columns of buttons and a gold trim to the forward and upper edge of the dolman collar. Contemporary sources show chevrons on the breeches. The officer's saddle cloth and sabretache are based on Mollo prints dated to 1798, as is the officer's shako. This was distinct in having a gilded metallic chin strap, metallic cockade and raquettes as well as one or two gold bands on the upper edge. Officers' plumes appear to have been black with a central yellow band. The Mollo prints also show officers armed with standard pattern hussar sabres with steel hilts although officers' sabres would have had brass hilts.

Austrian Hussar Uniforms at Marengo
Third Column Hussar Brigade
8th Nauendorf Hussars   Parrot Green Pelisse/dolman with Poppy red breeches
                        Black shako and yellow buttons
5th Hussars   Dark Green Pelisse/dolman with carmine breeches
                        Bright red shako and white buttons

General Numbsch's Hussar Brigade
9th Erdody Hussars   Dark Green Pelisse/dolman with carmine red breeches
                        Black shako and yellow buttons
7th Hussars   Light Blue Pelisse/dolman with Light Blue breeches
                        Grass green shako and white buttons

A surviving example of the ubiquitous Austrian 3-pounder which proved so deadly to the French at Marengo.

The French Army in 1800

Compared to the Armies of the Rhine and Danube on the German frontier, the French Army of Italy had always been a second-rate force. Throughout this period, France continued to maintain some 170-200,000 troops on its own borders, yet the Army of Italy barely reached 60,000 men.

Furthermore, after two years of campaign and successive defeats, the Army of Italy was in very poor condition. What survived in 1800 was a core of 30,000 men under the command of Generals Massena, Suchet and Soult. By April 1800, it was based along a southern mountainous frontline near Nice and a strip of land along the North-Western Italian coast leading to Genoa. The renewed Austrian offensive in 1800 culminating in the siege of Genoa all but completed its destruction. Massena's reports to Bonaparte paint a deeply pessimistic view of the army, which accords with Marbot's more vivid description:

'It was a mere shadow of an army. The troops, unpaid, almost without uniforms or shoes, were receiving only quarter rations, and dying of starvation, disease or epidemic, a consequence of long-term privations. The hospitals were full and without medicine or equipment. Units of soldiers, even whole regiments, were deserting every day to escape into France, over the Var bridge. They forced their way into Provence, saying they would only return once they were fed. Faced with this mass of misery, the Generals no longer had any authority.' Marbot

There is little doubt that Bonaparte and the French High Command viewed this army as posing a greater threat to the French themselves than to the Austrians. Low morale, desertion and mutiny was rife and Bonaparte was determined to keep it separate from his new Army of Reserve.

The Army of Reserve was created in 4 months. It took shape through a campaign of misinformation, secrecy and deception. Above all, Bonaparte wanted to hide the fact that he was marshalling a new invasion force. Drawn from regiments stationed all over France, including Paris, he sought to re-equip this force at break-neck speed, often whilst on the march. Chosen regiments were given orders to march directly to Geneva, by-passing large cities. The army gradually took shape as it converged in the Alpine passes. By April 1800, it could count on over 50,000 troops, almost twice the size of the Army of Italy.

The French had taken pains to gather low-grade garrison troops in Nice and Dijon, generating the false impression that the Army of Reserve was a third-rate force; this misinformation worked. The British and Austrians still expected the

French to invade from Nice, in an attempt to reinforce the Army of Italy. The real Army of Reserve came as a shock.

Overall, the Army was fresh and highly motivated, led by some of the best senior officers, under the command of Bonaparte. Unlike the Austrians, the French High Command was also very young. Bonaparte was 30 years old and other senior officers were mainly in their 30s and 40s; a large part of the army were veteran, young and professionally ambitious. In this respect, it had a towering advantage over the Austrians.

Yet it had fundamental weaknesses. Communications and supplies, stretching across the Alps, could not cope. It was desperately short of ammunition and artillery. The recent creation of an army transport corps had been a response to the collapse of the Commissary Service while crossing the Alps. The Commissary had always operated by hiring civilian transport and supply contractors. However, faced with the Alps, wagon drivers and mulateers simply deserted or refused to work for the Army – no matter what the pay. Amidst these precarious conditions, the Army could ill afford a long, drawn-out campaign. It needed to force the Austrians into a decisive battle and end the campaign before the Autumn rains closed the passes once again.

The army, drawn together at speed from so many disparate elements was a mixed bag. For one thing, not all the battalions marching into Italy had been re-equipped. Artists of the campaigns in 1800, like Kobell and Rugendas show French Consular troops dressed in a mix of old and new uniform styles, including many non-standard items. On the long marches to and through Italy, breeches, waistcoats and footwear were often replaced with whatever could be purchased or pillaged. Once in Italy, the army was no longer supplied with uniform items or arms and made do with what they had. Furthermore, the various divisions were usually kept apart on the march so that they could forage, bivouac and live off the land. They came together only when a battle was imminent.

The organisation of the French army was still very much influenced by the republican revolution. French regiments had been officially called demi-brigades under the influence of the revolution; demi-brigade was deemed to be a more populist term than 'regiment'. Two demi-brigades formed a 'brigade' which in turn was commanded by a General de Brigade. Two brigades formed a Division commanded by a General de Division. Finally, the highest level of Command was that of the Lieutenant-Generals. These were directly subordinate to the Commander in Chief and usually commanded two divisions and a brigade of cavalry. There were three Lieutenant-Generals at Marengo; Victor, Lannes and Desaix – all were to have key roles in the battle.

Despite the republican culture that still permeated the army, the demi-brigades functioned as regiments, just as in any standard army of the time. Each demi-brigade had 3 battalions which in turn were sub-divided into 6 companies, one of which was designated as a Grenadier Company. As in the Austrian army, the Grenadiers were the elite, picked from the tallest, most physically imposing recruits. As such, they often bore the brunt of the fighting. All other infantrymen were called fusiliers.

The French Infantry

Figure 28: Grenadier: Grenadier Company: 96th Demi-Brigade: Brigadier-General Rivaud's Division: Defence of Marengo.

Figure 29: Fusilier: 3rd Battalion: 44th Demi-Brigade: General Gardanne's Division: Front-line defence of Pietrabuona and Stortigliona farms

The 96th and 44th Demi-Brigades belonged to the two French divisions commanded by Lieutenant-General Victor, one of which formed the French front-line on the morning of the battle. Victor was to play one of the key roles in the battle and has left us a very vivid and detailed account of the events of that day. Victor's account is interesting in that he was not a life-long Bonapartist, siding with the restored monarchy in 1815. However, it was Victor who commanded the French demi-brigades for the first 4 hours of battle, whilst Bonaparte was bringing reinforcements from Torre Garofoli. He describes his initial positions at Pietrabuona as the battle commenced:

'General Victor placed several cannons along the front-line of his Advance-Guard Division and ordered General Gardanne to receive and resist the brunt of the enemy attack in the positions he held (at Pietrabuona). At about nine o'clock, O'Reilly's Austrians (Grenzer infantry) approached Pietrabuona and attempted to capture the position with the cannon fire of their artillery. However, our own artillery was able to respond very effectively, at first. The Austrian (Grenzers) then advanced to within musket range whilst the Line regiments of General Haddik formed up level with them. Our own men disrupted this advance by murderous volley fire, but finally the Austrians deployed for a general advance. With flags unfurled and regimental bands playing a rousing fanfare, they marched forward like a triumphal parade. They threatened to destroy the defending French by their overwhelming superiority.'

Victor

The first and most forward-placed French division comprised two demi-brigades, the 44th Demi-Brigade (1,750 men) and the 101st Demi-Brigade (1,500 men) under the command of General de Division, Gaspard Gardanne. Although nominally over 3,000 men strong, Gardanne's own account of the battle puts his force at no more than 2,000 infantry. This Division had been at the forefront of the assault that captured Marengo the evening before the battle. They now had to defend a front-line that stretched from the large farm-house buildings of Pietrabuona, 200m north of the Tortona road to La Stortigliona farm, some 700m to the south-east of the road. Like Marengo itself, both farms were large walled complexes made up of brick farm buildings and barns.

Some 800 metres behind this forward position, was the main French defensive line. This followed the arc of the narrow Fontanone drainage canal which ran about 100 m in front of the Marengo farm and its large walled courtyard. The canal dominated the main Tortona road, along which the Austrians planned to advance. The road crossed the canal over a narrow stone bridge, which the French had barricaded. However, the canal also ran alongside the road to the south at an oblique angle for several hundred metres. Behind this strong position was a second larger Division which formed part of Victor's Corps. This was made up of 3 demi-brigades; the 96th, 43rd and 24th Legere. On the day, all three were placed under the command of Brigadier-General Olivier Rivaud, after their own General de Division (Chambarlhac) fled the field early in the battle. On the morning of the battle, it was the 8,000 or so men of these five demi-brigades who held and defended Marengo for at least four hours until the arrival of reinforcements. These reinforcements would come from the Divisions of Lannes, Monnier and the Consular Guard.

The Austrians took several hours to deploy, commencing their attack at about 9am. After the initial Austrian artillery barrage and assault by the Grenzers of O'Reilly's Column, the 44th and 101st pulled back from Pietrabuona. They retreated, crossing the road bridge and redeploying along the Fontanone canal. Companies from two battalions (totalling about 500 men) from both the 44th and 101st remained on the east bank of the canal defending a southern flanking position at La Stortigliona farm.

'General Victor ordered Gardanne to conduct an ordered retreat en-echelon from the front-line at Pietrabuona. Having retreated, Gardanne's two regiments were to occupy an oblique line behind the Fontanone ditch; the left flank of this line

108 The French Army of Reserve

Figure 28

109 The French Army of Reserve

Figure 29

extended to the Bormida river whilst the right extended to Marengo, defending the roads and lines of communications which lay behind the village. One single battalion of the 101st was positioned to defend La Stortigliona farm.'
Victor

The renewed Austrian assault on Marengo itself only got under way after 10:30am. Victor says that it was the 44th and 101st who continued to defend the Fontanone for over an hour, before being relieved by the 96th, 43rd and 24th Legere under Rivaud. Shortly after midday, the French position at Marengo had been partly outflanked by Austrian fusiliers and Grenadiers: they had established a bridgehead across the ditch, 400m to the north, opposite Borbotta farm. The Austrians launched a succession of direct attacks on Marengo from the bridgehead and from the stone road-bridge. From this point on, Victor's demi-brigades were defending not only the Fontanone, but Marengo itself.

There are two key eyewitness accounts detailing the experience of these defending French infantrymen. The first is of Jean-Roche Coignet, at that time a young Grenadier in the 96th. The other was by Lt. General Victor himself: both are equally vivid. The defending troops of the 96th and 43rd had earned the nick-name 'Chambarlhac's brigands':

'All night we remained under arms. We placed outposts as far forward as possible and also placed small four-man pickets even further forward. At about two in the morning, two of these smaller pickets were over-run and the sentries killed. Our drums sounded the call to arms. It is difficult to convey the effect this had on us; it was like the sudden blast of a cannon. It seemed like the enemy was upon us. Lines were being formed across the entire plain and everything was in general commotion. I will never forget this moment, for at the time I was still a young, unseasoned recruit. Anyway, I have never pretended that the start of a battle ever inspired me with anything other than fear and dread.

At about 4 o'clock in the morning, the firing began. Aides from General Lannes assigned us a position in line of battle. We were ordered to retire behind a rise of ground in a field of high-standing wheat; here we waited, inactive for some time and partly concealed. All at once, we came under fire from both their artillery and their sharpshooters, firing from the willows and the marsh along the ditch. One shell exploded in our first company, killing seven men and a gendarme guarding General Chambarlhac; at this, our General fled and that was the last we saw of him that day.

Soon General Rivaud appeared, a small man with fine blonde moustaches; brave and active. His horse had already been killed, so he approached Colonel

Lepraux on foot and asked where Chambarlac was. On the Colonel's reply, he announced that he would take command of the division. He immediately ordered our Company of Grenadiers to advance in an extended line and open fire on the enemy. He ordered; "Advance and do not halt whilst reloading your muskets – you will be recalled when I decide." The remainder of our battalions were formed up, behind us, as we advanced.

As we approached, the Austrians emerged from the willows, formed up in front of us and fired at us in volleys. Our little General also ordered our own battalions to fire from our rear. There, we were sacrificed, caught between two deadly fires. I found myself running behind the trunk of a tall willow tree, from where I continued to fire as best I could. However, the fire was so heavy that I soon had to throw myself to the ground, covering my head; I thought I was going to die. Bullets and grape-shot showered from every direction, destroying the tree and covering me in leaves and branches. In this encounter, the majority of my Grenadier Company were killed or wounded; of our 170 Grenadiers, only 14 remained. Fortunately for me, our division advanced by battalions and I was able to join another company of our battalion; I remained with this company for the rest of the day.

We soon fell back to defend our original position, under constant canister and grape-shot fire. Our battalions held the front-line on the left-flank (southern flank) of the army, alongside the main road to Alessandria. Here, we faced the heaviest fighting. In their efforts to gain control of the road, the enemy constantly tried to outflank us; and we had to guard our left to prevent them from surrounding us. The powder smoke was so thick, you could barely see yourself.'
Coignet

What Coignet did not fully appreciate was that the battle had already been lost elsewhere; the right and centre of the French position, stretching from Marengo to Castel Ceriolo had begun to collapse. General Victor's account is very clear in the timings and sequences of this stage of the battle, details which only he could have known. Between midday and 1pm, the Austrians managed to both outflank Marengo from the north and attack it directly from two bridgeheads established across the Fontanone:

'*Under covering fire of grapeshot and canister from 30 cannons, the enemy had established a bridging point directly opposite Marengo. General Lattermann raced across this with 3,000 of his grenadiers and attempted to take Marengo by storm. Three times, our troops had to retreat and three times they counter-attacked to force the enemy back. We pushed them back as far as the other side of the Fontanone and there both sides fired at each other at point blank range for over a quarter of an hour. By this time, half the combatants were dead with both*

banks covered in corpses and wounded. General Rivaud too was wounded by shrapnel in the thigh, but he was determined to hold on to the last extremity, knowing that losing Marengo would mean losing the battle...
The enemy who had not been able to dislodge us with the elite of their infantry now tried to commit their dragoons. These too charged in a mass but were also forced to retreat under our intense fire, leaving 60 casualties behind. The Austrians reinforced their grenadiers and for a fourth time they attempted a frontal assault, attacking both Rivaud's men and the 40th Line, our final reserve. Our battalions now collapsed and began to retreat and all seemed lost until Rivaud ordered his drummers to beat the charge and once again our troops managed to push back this fourth attack, pushing the enemy back some 300 feet from Marengo...but our losses had been great and our numerical inferiority now showed...We'd run out of ammunition and most of our cannons were destroyed. At this point, many of our skirmishers, who'd run out of cartridges, began to retreat. At this, the Austrians pushed forward once again with General Bellegarde's men overwhelming the centre while a powerful division of enemy troops threatened our flanks. Our soldiers finally began to fall back. We had held on to our positions for 6 hours and we feared that to persevere in this would lead to either disorder or a complete rout.
At this point, Generals Victor and Lannes judged that it was better to use what little remained to them in men and ammunition to retreat towards our promised reinforcements. They ordered a full retreat.'
Victor

Figure 29 shows the standard Fusilier uniform of 1799-1800. The uniform was based on the long-tailed blue coat. Dyed in the republican tricolore colours of blue white and red, it was also called the 'Habit Francais'. It had lapels with 7 buttons on each lapel, though the coat itself was fastened by hooks and eyes down the middle. The brass buttons bore the demi-brigade number. The cut of the Habit coat changed little over the period 1795-1805, though the width of the lapels gradually widened. In 1800, lapels were still usually quite narrow, particularly on infantry coats, appearing more like the infantry coats of the mid-1700s. Turn-backs are always shown plain white, piped red, in this period. Collars, cuffs and shoulder straps were coloured and piped as in Figure 29, though there were variations in the cut and colour of the cuff flap; however, sources suggest that in this earlier period the norm was either red cuff flaps or no cuff flaps at all. Rear pockets on each coat tail were also piped red and could be either vertical or horizontal.

Headgear was a felt bicorn with a tricolore cockade fixed with yellow braid to a brass button; a pompom was also worn. Pompoms could be round or lozenge-shaped and either single colours or in tricolore colours. Contemporary depictions show the pre-1801 bicorns as shorter and deeper in cross-section than those worn from 1801-1806; they were closer in cut to the tricorns worn in the 1700s. The bicorn could be worn with the point facing forward 'in marching order' (as in Figure 28) or side-on 'in battle order' (as in Figure 29). Bicorns were made from felt, which contained a significant element of new-world beaver fur, and were meant to be relatively water-resistant; there were no standard-issue waterproof covers.

Whatever the regulations prescribed, this is often where the standardized element of the uniform ended for the mass of line infantry. In the early Italian campaigns, the Habit coat and bicorn was sometimes the only standard item of uniform worn by an infantry starved of supplies. Pictorial sources show that French infantry in Italy wore whatever supplies came to hand.

The fusilier (in theory) was not permitted to carry the 73cm 'briquet' short sword. Therefore, he only had one 9cm-wide cross-belt for a standard black cartridge-case, passing over the left shoulder; this belt also carried a loop for the bayonet scabbard. He also wore a waistcoat under his blue coat; this was actually a woollen all-purpose jacket with sleeves, also worn for fatigue duties. Although it became standardized as a white jacket with a single row of buttons, the 1790s witnessed a plethora of forms, from striped waistcoats to double breasted waistcoats (as in Fig 28).

In theory, legwear comprised white breeches and black buttoned gaiters which covered the knee, with white gaiters worn in summer. However, the memoires of the infantryman Elzear Blaze are quite emphatic in asserting that these gaiters and breeches were thrown away once a campaign started, being replaced by non-regulation trousers. In 1800, these 'fatigue' trousers often appear to have been supplied (at least in part) by the army itself, as they are often shown white and striped in a variation of red and blue stripes. Infantry shoes did not last long, and Fig 29 wears non-regulation footwear; even Grenadier Coignet says that his newly issued shoes were already destroyed after crossing the Alps.

The over-riding impression of contemporary visual and written sources was of an army where irregular clothing formed a large part of the uniform. This was exacerbated under the pressures of campaign, where soldiers bivouacked in the open for weeks on end, without regular supplies. Although, Bonaparte made strenuous efforts to reclothe and re-equip his new Army of Reserve in the weeks leading up to the crossing of the Alps, even elite units like the 9th Legere arrived at the Alps with old out-dated uniforms.

Standard equipment included a calf-skin knapsack and various versions of the excellent 1777-model Charleville musket. Non-standard equipment included water containers like flasks or gourds and cooking implements.

Figure 28 wears the standard Grenadier uniform of the republican and early consular army. The main distinction for Grenadiers was a red falling plume attached to the bicorn; red epaulettes were also worn. However, throughout this early period, Grenadier epaulettes are always shown partially fastened and pushed back at an angle behind the shoulders. Two red-cloth grenade-badges were sewn onto the white coat-turn-backs. A brass grenade badge also adorned the cartridge case. The other main distinction was a second cross-belt passing over the right shoulder, on which the briquet short sword was carried.

Coignet's memoires offer a superb view of the battle as seen from the point of view of a French infantryman. His own eyewitness experience of the battle also appears to be reliable in that it accords with other information on the battle. Considerably less reliable are his comments on what is happening in other parts of the battle; for example, his summary of the fighting around the courtyard of Marengo itself which he could not have witnessed. One should take a critical approach in reading the memoires, particularly when he comments on events that don't relate to his own actual experience.

Figure 30: Grenadier Sergeant: Grenadier Company: 28th Demi-Brigade: General Watrin's Division commanded by Lt. General Lannes: Defence of right flank to the north of Marengo.

Figure 31: Fusilier: 1st Battalion: 70th Demi-Brigade: Brigadier -General Monnier's Division: Counter-attack on Castel-Ceriolo

Figure 32: Tirailleur: 1st Battalion: 59th Demi-Brigade: General Guenand's Brigade: Final French counter-attack

Bonaparte had discounted any possibility that the Austrians would attack at Marengo and consequently French forces were dispersed over a wide area on the day of the battle. When the Austrians attacked, the French were completely wrong-footed. As the bulk of the French army hurried towards the battlefield on the 14th June, they had no choice but to be fed piecemeal into the fighting, sometimes as whole divisions, as brigades or even single regiments. However, they failed to do anything other than delay the inexorable Austrian advance. It was the Austrians who maintained the initiative throughout the day, until the arrival of Desaix.

The French reinforcements arrived during the course of the afternoon and joined battle in three main groups; Lannes' Division shortly after 1 o'clock, Monnier's Division after 2 o'clock and finally Desaix's troops at about 5.30pm.

The first to arrive between 1-1:30pm were the four demi-brigades of Lannes' Division; these included the 22nd, 40th and 28th Demi-Brigades and the 6th Legere.* Of these, it was the 28th Demi-Brigade which took up a defensive position on the far northern flank of the French army. Over the following two hours, these 5,000 infantrymen fought a rearguard defensive action against Ott's Second Column advancing from Castel Ceriolo and against Austrian infantry trying to cross the Fontanone; fighting in the same area as the Consular Guard. Commanding Lannes' largest brigade was Brigadier-General Watrin. General Watrin's report to Berthier describes a front line that ran for 3km from the Tortona road to Castel Ceriolo.

'We had for a long time maintained our positions inflicting high casualties on the enemy. I now realised that the enemy had arrived in force at Castel Ceriolo and was about to deploy a strong column on my right flank. I sent a battalion of the 22nd to reinforce the 6th legere, which had already been outflanked by this strong enemy force which was now overwhelming our troops. General Lannes supported this move, by advancing the 28th towards the same area, while the 40th defended itself against a number of charges made by the Austrian cavalry along the main road from Marengo'
Watrin's report to Berthier

The second group of reinforcements arrived about an hour later between 2.00 and 3.00pm. This last group included the 800 men of the Consular Guard and about 3,500 infantry of the three demi-brigades of General Monnier's Division; the 70th, 72nd and 19th Legere. These demi-brigades arrived with Bonaparte himself. He immediately sent them to counterattack the same northern flank, anxious to secure the French line of retreat. Although Ott's troops prevailed once again, these two French counterattacks slowed down Ott's advance and ensured that by late afternoon, Ott's troops were as exhausted as the rest of the Austrian army. Watrin's 40% casualties testify to the intensity of the fighting in the northern plain.

'The division sustained 13 officers killed and 83 wounded and a further 2,000 casualties amongst killed, wounded and captured. We suffered greatly from enemy artillery fire which caused the greater part of our casualties. Mon General, I apologise for the disorder of my report, which is occasioned by the suffering I have experienced at the death of my own brother, killed whilst leading the 22nd.'
Watrin's report to Berthier

116   The French Army of Reserve

Figure 30

117 The French Army of Reserve

Figure 31

Figure 32

Between 2.30 and 3.00pm, the entire French front line was in a state of collapse. Grenadier Coignet's account describes a confused and often desperate retreat, where different units ran out of ammunition, under the pressure of sustained Austrian cavalry assaults. Coignet's retreat with the 96th would have been further to the south of the battlefield, parallel with the main Tortona road.

'Although we maintained our positions (behind the Fontanone), enemy shells had set fire to the wheat fields around us, causing the discarded cartridge cases to explode. This disordered our ranks considerably and it took all the energy of our officers to keep us together. Over time, the enemy artillery fire began to overwhelm us and our position got steadily worse. We could see our ranks visibly thinning. All around us we could see only the wounded and their comrades carrying them to the ambulance; these men did not return. While we were losing men, we could see the Austrians constantly receiving fresh reinforcements. No one came to reinforce us. Behind us the plain was covered with the dying and the men who carried them. Also, as our muskets began to overheat and foul through overuse, we could no longer push the cartridges down the barrels. Our desperate officers ordered us to piss down the barrels and dry them by burning loose powder; however our ammunition was also running out and we had now lost our ambulance. At this point, we beat the retreat which began in good order. About 600 men of the Consular Guard arrived carrying cartridges in blankets slung across their shoulders, which they distributed passing behind our ranks. We were once again able to renew our fire. By then, we had reached the middle of the plain, having retreated a long way. We passed yet more willows, more drainage ditches and scattered hedges…
The Austrian dragoons charged us and broke through our forward platoons, sabring us. I received a sword blow to the back of my head, which was so powerful, it cut my hair queue clean off. I was lucky I had probably the thickest queue in the regiment; it needed a yard of black ribbon and half a pound of powder to dress. It saved my life. The blow cut clean through my coat collar and through one of my epaulettes, but left me with a flesh wound. Nevertheless, it knocked me down and I rolled into a ditch, dazed. While I lay there Kellermann's cavalry charged and retreated three times, passing over me. When I regained consciousness, I threw away my cartridge case and sabre and seized the tail of a French dragoon's horse, as it retreated. I took great strides trying to keep up as the horse pulled me along, but soon collapsed exhausted, unable to breathe. Thank God, I found myself carried to our French lines. I soon found a new musket, cartridge case and sack, as the ground was covered with them; and I joined the ranks of the Second Grenadier Company of the 96th regiment.'

Coignet

The pristinely uniformed French infantryman sometimes shown in officially commissioned paintings simply did not exist in reality – at least not in the 1800 campaign. Some cavalry regiments and the Guard would have been well equipped, but the mass of infantry were not. Once their standard issue shoes and legwear wore out, within the first few weeks of campaign, they wore anything they could find.

The uniform of the Grenadier in Figure 30 is a case in point and serves to show details that can be found in many contemporary prints and paintings.** The Grenadier Sergeant wears an earlier shorter pattern of bearskin, similar to those worn before the revolution. Although not officially part of the Grenadier uniform, bearskins were traditional, valuable and usually the reserve of NCOs; these short-pattern bearskins continued to be worn throughout the consulate. The Grenadier's falling red plume is also worn with a second tricolore plume. Although still worn throughout 1799-1800, republican symbols like tricolore plumes and sashes rapidly fell out of favour under the consulate. On campaign in Italy, the Habit-coat was often worn unfastened and the epaulettes were always worn pushed back behind the shoulders. The striped waistcoat, often double-breasted was so common as to be considered standard issue. Legwear and footwear were also commonly non-regulation. The Grenadier's NCO status is marked by the double gold bars above the cuff.

Figure 31 shows a fusilier of the 70th demi-brigade. His Habit-coat has the thin style of lapels common to troops prior to 1800. Although he has 3 large regulation buttons below the right lapel; these were often missing in coats of the time. Pockets could be either horizontal (Fig 31) or vertical (Fig30) and cuff flaps could be either scalloped (Fig 30) or straight (Fig 31) or absent (Fig 28). The fusilier has been supplied with non-regulation striped breeches and short white gaiters; both common items.

Figure 32 shows a skirmisher of the 59th Demi-Brigade. French Line demi-brigades had already developed an organized system of detaching skirmishers as an advance line in front of the battalion. It wasn't until 1804, that these specialist troops were organized into new elite 'Voltigeur' companies, with special uniform distinctions. However, the regular Line demi-brigades of the Republic already had select skirmishers in their ranks, sometimes informally referred to as tirailleurs or even chasseurs. Indeed, it was the withdrawal of these skirmishers that sparked off the general retreat from the front-line at Marengo. Based on pictorial sources like the Rovatti manuscript or the Langendijk paintings, at least some of these skirmishers already wore green plumes and green epaulettes. ***

*These timings are based on those given in the accounts of General Victor and Stutterheim. Although rough estimates, they accord with most other reliable sources
**These details are shown in pictorial sources by Zix, Seele, Rugendas, Landolt, Hauck, Langendyck and Rottmann as well as prints like the Zurich and Augsberger manuscripts.
***The Rovatti manuscript shows a line infantry skirmisher (Rovatti uses the term chasseur) from the 47th Demi-Brigade wearing line infantry uniform with green epaulettes and plume.

Demi-brigades at Marengo

1. Defending Marengo: Under the command of Lieutenant General Victor
Gardanne's Division
- 44th Ligne   3 Btn   1,750 men
- 101st Ligne   3 Btn   1,890

(Olivier) Rivaud's Division (Chambarlhac)
- 43rd Ligne   3 Btn   1,900 men
- 96th Ligne   3 Btn   1,590
- 24th Legere   3 Btn   1,800

2. Reinforcing northern flank of Marengo: Under the command of Lieutenant General Lannes
These troops arrived during the course of the early afternoon.

Watrin's Division
- 28th Ligne   3 Btn   1,000 men
- 22nd Ligne   3 Btn   1,260
- 40th Ligne   3 Btn   1,720
- 6th Legere   3 Btn   1,110

3. Counter-attacking on northern flank of Battlefield: Under the command of the First Consul, Napoleon Bonaparte
These troops arrived during mid-afternoon, just as the French retreat commenced

Monnier's Division
- 70th Ligne   3 Btn   1,460 men
- 72nd Ligne   3 Btn   1,240
- 19th Legere   2 Btn   910

4. Counter-attacking at Cascina Grossa: Under the command of Lieutenant General Desaix
These troops arrived at about 5 o'clock and deployed for action shortly before 6 o'clock

Boudet's Division
- 30th Ligne   3 Btn   1,430 men
- 59th Ligne   3 Btn   1,870
- 9th Legere   3 Btn   2,010

Figure 33: Chasseur: 24ᵗʰ Legere: Chambarlhac's Division under command of General Rivaud: Defence of Marengo.

Figure 34: Chasseur: 1ˢᵗ Legere: General Lapoype's Division: Not present at the battle.

Figure 35: Corporal Carabinier: Carabinier Company: 9ʰ Legere: General Boudet's Division under the command of Lieutenant-General Desaix: Final French Counter-attack

The Legere demi-brigades were the light infantry demi-brigades of the French army. In the Army of Reserve, each Division usually comprised two 'Demi-Brigade de Bataille' and one 'Demi-Brigade Legere'. The role of these line and light infantry demi-brigades had become increasingly blurred, as line units also developed their own skirmishing troops. However, the Legere units tended to view themselves as elite soldiers, able to take on the full range of light infantry roles; the reality is that their unit reputations varied considerably.

At one end of the scale were the 24ᵗʰ Legere. According to Coignet, this demi-brigade had shot many of their own officers the day before Marengo. Mutiny and mutinous incidents were not uncommon in the Army of Reserve. Particularly as many of these units had been over-stretched and poorly supplied throughout the campaign; the 12ᵗʰ Hussars had also mutinied. According to Coignet, Napoleon's response was to deliberately expose the demi-brigade to enemy attack. Its ranks were more than decimated. A mutiny that was never officially recorded received a similarly unofficial punishment. Grenadier Coignet's notebooks are the only source to directly mention it:*

'On the 12ᵗʰ our two other demi-brigades (the 24ᵗʰ Legere and 43ʳᵈ Ligne) came to support our right flank and our division was once again reunited. Someone told us the village in front of us was called Marengo. In the morning, the drums beat the call to breakfast. What joy! Seventeen wagons of bread had arrived. What happiness for men who were starving! We rushed towards the convoy. What disappointment! The bread was mouldy and blue – but we ate it nonetheless.

On the 13ᵗʰ, at the break of day, we were ordered to advance on to a great plain and at about 2 o'clock we formed in battle order. Aides de Camp arrived from our right and raced in all directions carrying orders; and so, every battalion was set in motion. Then the 24ᵗʰ Legere was sent forward apparently on reconnaissance. The 24ᵗʰ Legere advanced quite far ahead of us and on making contact with the enemy became involved in very heavy fighting, sustaining heavy casualties. This demi-brigade was forced to form square to defend itself.

Yet Bonaparte had intentionally placed it in this terrible position. It was claimed that he wanted the demi-brigade to be destroyed. Here's why. When the 24th Legere was ordered to advance under fire by General Lannes at the battle of Montebello, they began by shooting their own officers. The soldiers spared only one lieutenant. I don't really know the reason for this terrible act of revenge. The Consul, informed of what had happened, hid his indignation. He could do nothing, now that we were faced with the enemy. The lieutenant who had survived the murder of his comrades was promoted to captain; new officers were appointed. Nevertheless, everyone knew that Bonaparte had forgotten nothing. It was not until about five or six o'clock in the evening that we were finally sent forward to assist the 24th Legere. When we arrived, the soldiers and officers heaped insults on us. They shouted that we had intentionally abandoned them to have their throats cut by the enemy, as if it was our fault. I estimate they lost half their men. Yet, they fought bravely enough on the following day.
Coignet - notebooks

It is notable that battle honours for this demi-brigade were not submitted; there were no officially recognised acts of bravery in this unit.

The 1st and 9th Legere were both prestigious units with well-established reputations. The 1st Legere was part of General Lapoype's Division which should have been marching towards Marengo. It is a measure of Bonaparte's complacency that he ordered Lapoype to return north and recross the Po river. On the day of the battle, the 1st Legere together with the rest of Lapoype's Division was some 24km to the north-east, close to Castel Nuovo; too far to be recalled.

The 9th Legere played perhaps the single most critical role in the entire battle. The actions of the 9th Legere certainly saved the French from defeat and may well have saved Bonaparte's political career. Napoleon recognised this and ensured that they were given the semi-formal title of 'L'incomparable'.

Arriving late in the day towards 6 o'clock, Lieutenant-General Desaix lined the 9th Legere behind the trees and hedges of the road leading to the village of Cascina Grossa. This road is the present day *Via della Liberta*, which connects

---

*This incident is only recorded in the first published editions of Coignet's notebooks from the 1850s to 1880s. It was edited out of later editions. Furthermore, Coignet's first editor later inserted a note to say that the paragraph, although added by the author himself, was not recorded in the hand-written manuscript. The only corroborating evidence is that the 24th Legere were denied formal battle honours, though this may be coincidence.

124   The French Army of Reserve

Figure 33

125 The French Army of Reserve

Figure 34

126 The French Army of Reserve

Figure 35

the main Tortona road to Cascina Grossa. Desaix placed the 30th and 59th Demi-Brigades to the north of this intersection, similarly shielded behind a line of orchards and vineyards. At this point, Desaix's 5-6,000 infantry probably outnumbered the Austrian column advancing towards them.   This final counterattack had all the hall-marks of an ambush. Whatever the intention may have been, the counterattack succeeded beyond even Bonaparte's expectations.

'The 9th Legere arrived along the same road from Alessandria, alongside which we had been fighting since the morning. By then, our regiment had reached the very end of the Marengo plain and we were on an area of raised ground from which we could see the 9th below us, advancing like a forest of bayonets. As for the Austrians, who were still some way behind us they were deceived by the rise of the ground, and did not suspect the arrival of our reinforcements. For Desaix's men now found a terrain which seemed to have been chosen in advance. To their left rose a gigantic hedge of trees, perpendicular to the main road and protected by a kind of embankment; behind which all the troops took cover, concealed. Once in position, even the cavalry were hidden from view.

The Austrians followed us as if they were strolling in to camp, guns balanced on their shoulders. They no longer took any notice of us, believing we were in complete rout. By now, we had passed Desaix's men by about 300 paces, and the Austrians were about to reach (this line of trees). At this very moment we heard the command: 'Battalion fire – oblique to the right!'

The head of the Austrian column were hit as if by lightning, as grapeshot and shells rained down on them. The charge sounded. Each one of us turned and began to run forward; we didn't shout, we screamed! The brave men of the 9th leaped through the hedges and attacked these Hungarian grenadiers with bayonets; the enemy had no time to recover. The 30th and 59th Line advanced at the same time and our cavalry struck the final blow… from that moment, the battle turned in our favour. Nevertheless, as we began to advance once more, we were attacked by enemy troops; we crossed bayonets and forced them to flee. Here I received another head wound, parrying the bayonet of an Austrian grenadier. As I parried his weapon, the point of his bayonet caught me just above my eye. My own strike did not miss. Nevertheless, my eye was covered in blood. I carried on walking and did not feel the pain. By now, our position had changed considerably. We had advanced across about three quarters of the plain and in front of us the enemy were in complete collapse. Infantrymen, cavalry, wagons and artillery – everything was in chaos. A pitiful sight. We pursued them until nine o'clock in the evening.'
Coignet

The uniforms worn by Figures 33-35 serve to show both the standard and non-regulation elements of the Legere uniform. The one standard item was the light infantry coat, which in essence was the same blue light-infantry coat that continued throughout the Napoleonic period, with minor modifications. In 1800, it was already piped white, short-tailed with blue turn-backs. The lapels were cut differently to lapels on standard line-infantry coats, with the base merging directly into the fold of the coat. Buttons were either white metal or brass but cuffs and cuff flaps ranged from red to blue. A white hunting horn badge is usually shown on the turnbacks. Collars were nearly always red. Other standard equipment included two cross-straps, one for the cartridge case and one for the briquet short-sword.

Figure 35 shows a Sergeant of Carabiniers of the 9th Legere. The uniform follows the commissioned painting by Lejeune, completed a year after the battle. It is a uniform that became the basis for a more standardized light infantry uniform under the consulate, also depicted by Hoffmann. However, General Boudet's letters show that it may not have been the uniform set out in the regulations before 1800. Furthermore, as late as the beginning of May, the 9th Legere had still not been issued with new uniforms. A mere six weeks before the battle, they paraded in front of the Consul at Dijon, dressed in a tattered mix of clothing:

'It was the turn of Boudet's division to be inspected. They were paraded at eight o'clock in the morning on soggy ground in the pouring rain. The 30th Line were without shoes and the 59th were without bayonets. As they arrived in front of the 9th Legere, the Consul frowned.
The regulation uniform of the troops of this regiment was:
-A light blue coat with lapels; buff facings with white buttons; white waistcoat, double breasted with two rows of buttons; white trousers; half-gaiters in cloth; a tall round hat with a small brim, widening slightly at the top, wrapped in a sash of bearskin (a flamme); one side of the hat being slightly rolled-up; attached to which was a sky-blue plume with a black tip. Instead of wearing such a uniform, three quarters of the men were dressed in a kind of jacket in blue or brown calico, covering a tattered waistcoat and shirt; striped fatigue trousers; no gaiters, but only shreds of canvas to tighten the lower legs; sandals instead of shoes; old fatigue cap-bonnets instead of hats. In this outfit, and in the torrential rain, the soldiers looked a sorry sight.'
Letter of General Boudet in Gachot

Bonaparte threatened the Commissary officer with the firing squad if the regiment was not reclothed within 3 days. Whether the 9th Legere troops were re-equipped is not known, but many of the troops crossing the Alps did so in old-issue uniforms. The Carabiniers were the elite companies of the Legere battalions; the equivalent of grenadiers. The uniform of the carabinier in Figure 35 is marked by a carabinier's red falling plume and red carabinier epaulettes, worn pushed back behind the shoulders. He wears a new issue shako, which became standardized after 1801. Like most light infantry shakos of the consular period, it has a brass lozenge plate, embossed with a hunting horn and the regimental number. Lejeune shows the 9th wearing long cavalry-style overall trousers, complete with a buttoned red side-stripe; these are shown being worn over the top of the shoes; they were not worn with gaiters. Cuffs and cuff flaps were red, as depicted by Lejeune. However, the majority of light-Infantrymen in each demi-brigade were Chasseurs. The chasseurs constituted five sixths of each battalion; these more numerous chasseurs wore green epaulettes.

If Figure 35 shows the new style of uniform that began to be introduced under the consulate, Figure 33 shows the type of uniform probably worn by the majority of light infantrymen on campaign before 1801. It is a style of uniform shown by nearly all contemporary artists throughout the 1799-1800 campaign, including Kobell, Rugendas, Seele and Lejeune himself. The Light infantry coat, although standardized, could vary in its shade of blue-dye and included versions which were light blue.* Other elements of dress borrowed heavily from that of the light cavalry hussars, with whom the Legere identified. The head-dress could be either a mirliton** or an early version shako; either would invariably be covered by a sash of material called a 'flamme' or 'wing'. By the late 1790s, these make-shift head-dresses usually had a piece of leather or material tied to the front to form a sun-visor or peak. The red and black plume on Figure 33 is based on a Rugendas print of 1799.

Cavalry-style side-buttoned overall trousers were commonly worn; these were often striped either with horizontal or vertical blue or red stripes. Rugendas also shows French Legere troops wearing versions of these trousers with side buttons only up to the knee; they were often tight-fitting like Hungarian infantry trousers.

The uniform worn by the 1st Legere Chasseur in Figure 34 is taken from the Zurich manuscript datable to 1799-1800. The Chasseur wears a regulation Legere uniform, including blue breeches and waistcoat, and short white summer issue gaiters. Nevertheless, he still wears a version of the old light infantry leather casquet, commonly worn before 1799. This is not the only source to show this older form of head-dress still being worn in this period; Kobell shows 3 light-infantrymen in 1800 in the Army of the Rhine also wearing the casquet. However, it serves to underline the varied, non-standard forms of Legere uniforms in 1800; the combined result of irregular supplies and irregular traditions.

Twelve honorary muskets were awarded to soldiers in the 9th Legere. The citations give some idea of the type of fighting these men were involved in. Half of the citations were for sharpshooters (tirailleur) and most of the citations mention fighting against Austrian cavalry.

Jacques: sergeant: *Whilst leading the tirailleurs, his men were attacked by enemy cavalry who were attempting to charge the battalion. He shot several cavalrymen, dismounting them and deterring the others from charging.*
Mahut*: corporal of grenadiers (carabiniers): When he saw the enemy about to capture one of our dragoon officers, he killed one of the enemy and caused the others to flee. On capturing the enemy's horse, he was shot and wounded.*
Piessevauxx*: chasseur: Detached as a tirailleur and attacked by two Hungarian hussars. He wounded one and forced the other to retreat. At the same time, he was charged by 6 Austrian cavalrymen who sabred him several times, leaving him for dead. He then rose from the point where they had left him and ran towards a fleeing enemy grenadier, catching him and taking him prisoner.*

(*Earlier coats from 1796 are shown light blue with dark blue turn-backs, dark blue with light blue turn-backs and even red piping.)
(**a simple felt pointed cap worn by the hussars)

Figure 36: Sous-Lieutenant: 6th Legere: General Lannes' Division: Defending northern flank of Marengo.

Figure 37: Senior Officer of Commissary: Army of Reserve.

Figure 36 and 37 shows the uniform styles of two very different types of officer.

Figure 36 is a lower rank Sous-Lieutenant in the 6th Legere. There are many good contemporary sources for light infantry officers' uniforms including Vernet, Hoffman, Rovatti and Lejeune, as well as the Zurich manuscript. Lejeune in particular shows 9th Legere officers at the battle still wearing bicorns. Officers' side-arms included epees in the Line-infantry and sabres in the Light-infantry. Hair was always worn queued. Officer status was marked by silver or gold epaulettes (depending on the button colour) and a gorget. Junior officers wore only one fringed-epaulette on the left shoulder and a contre-epaulette on the right. This officer's bicorn has gold corner-pompoms and a gold-thread tie. He

also wears tall riding boots, folded down to allow him to march; strap-on spurs would be unbuckled when marching.
Junior officers included the ranks of Adjutant, Sous-Lieutenant, Lieutenant and Captain, in that order. Senior officers from Major to Colonel wore epaulettes with heavy silver or gold bullion fringes.

The 6th Legere was heavily committed in the front-line, north of Marengo, close to Castel Ceriolo. They fought to maintain control of the northern part of the Fontanone and counterattacked towards Castel Ceriolo itself. Throughout the day, they attacked and retreated across the fields and vineyards of the northern part of the plain. Their list of battle honours gives a vivid account of the type of fighting their men experienced:
6th LIGHT.—15 Honour Rifles.
MANSUIS (Claude), Chasseur.—Received a ball in the right side at the beginning of the affair, and continued to fight until the end, although his captain had several times invited him to retire.
DAUMAS (Benoît), Corporal —Having asked his captain's permission to move forward, he fired on an enemy battalion commander, cut him down, and thus deprived the troop of its leader, which gave way immediately.
JAVOT (André), Chasseur.—Having had his knapsack carried off by cannonball and been knocked to the floor – he had the presence of mind to await the approach of an enemy horseman, shoot him down with his musket at point blank range and mount his horse, riding it back to his company.
LEVERT (Francois), Corporal.—He summoned thirty Austrians defending a farm building to surrender; on their refusal, he rushed to the door, broke it in with his rifle butt and by his brave action, took them all prisoner.
TISSOT (Jacques), Corporal.— Left behind and isolated, he awaited two enemy horsemen who had pursued him for some time. He killed one with a musket shot, and took the other prisoner after having wounded him with the bayonet.
PUISSANT (Jean), Carabinier.—As one of fifteen skirmishers appointed to flush out an almost equal number of Austrians, he threw himself first into a very deep ditch that had to be crossed, and encouraged his comrades to follow him, with the result that they succeeded in driving out the enemy.
LANGLOIS (Alphonse), Sergeant.—After having obtained the authorization of his chef de bataillon, he took up a concealed position in some vines, fired on an enemy lieutenant-colonel of cavalry, and shattered his shoulder: five horsemen charged him at once; he escaped them, without abandoning his weapon, despite the difficulty he had in carrying it out of the vines.
GAULLIER (François), Sergeant.—Was in command of ten chasseurs detached as skirmishers, when he found himself cut off from his battalion. His unit was

132   The French Army of Reserve

Figure 37

Figure 36

charged by about 100 enemy cavalrymen: he led his unit to the shelter of a ruined farmbuilding, which he defended, refusing to surrender.

The Commissary senior officer in Figure 37 is based on two prints; one by Labrousse of an officer of the Commissary in the late 1790s and the other by Hoffman painted in the late Consulate. Figure 37 is based on the earlier source. He wears a single-breasted surtout coat with the turn-backs opened out. The red cuffs and falling collar are edged with leaf-design gold brocade. Both officers have tricolore plumes, common throughout the army.

The military supply system under the republic was run by the Commissary who, in turn, commissioned civilian contractors to both supply the army and to deliver those supplies. There was no military supply system other than contractors and even the Artillery Train was a newly created service, still in its early infancy. The system was notoriously corrupt and ineffective; particularly for the army of Italy. However, being an Officer of the Commissary was not an easy job, particularly when the commanding general was Bonaparte. Bonaparte characteristically pushed his army to breaking point and the first thing to break was always the Commissarial Supply system. Sources from the time testify how the supply service had reached crisis point even before the crossing of the Alps. Bonaparte was very aware that supplies would fail. However, he was a calculating risk taker and was willing to take this risk. He was also a tireless organiser, improving the system in a very short amount of time. Commissary officers who did not measure up, were given short shrift. Bonaparte's reaction to the poor state of the 9th Legere in May 1800 shows how he approached this ever-present and very significant problem; employing a mix of tough leadership and inspired rhetoric:

'*In their tattered outfits, and in the torrential rain, the soldiers of the 9th Legere looked a sorry sight.*
"Citizen Ricard!" exclaimed the First Consul. 'Y*ou were appointed on 9 Germinal as commissioner of clothing. Forty days later, on 28 Floréal, I am presented with troops covered in rags. Do you expect me to ask the men of the 9th to cross the eternal ice* of the *Alps dressed like this?*
'But Citizen Consul, the stores…
Bonaparte waved his whip and looked livid.
'*The stores are full. You have in Lyon 8,000 uniforms and carts for transport. Don't interrupt me, citizen! With this level of negligence, the General ought to have you shot. Go away now; today is the 17th - if on the 20th the Boudet division is not better dressed, never dare to reappear before me again.*'

When the division was formed in a semi-circle, the Consul asked to address them: "The fields of Italy," he said, "will be, for you, a storehouse of plenty. I've already told some of you this four years ago. In these fields, an arrogant enemy awaits us. You are, just like your predecessors who followed me at Lodi and Montenotte, badly dressed, badly fed and still unpaid. In fifteen days, all this will be changed. Soldiers, I will ask of you one great effort before you meet with the Austrians. Follow me with confidence and you will return covered in glory, having saved our country, which is once again threatened by foreign hordes." With the inspection complete, Bonaparte climbed into his carriage hitched to horses belonging to the artillery and returned very quickly to Dijon.
Letter of General Boudet in Gachot

Figure 38: Corporal: Grenadiers a pied: Garde des Consuls: General Bessieres: Counter-attack towards Castel Ceriolo

Figure 39: Drummer: Grenadiers a pied: Garde des Consuls:

Figure 40: Chasseur: Chasseur a pied: Garde des Consuls: General Bessieres: Counter-attack towards Castel Ceriolo

Figure 41: Sapper: Chasseur a pied: Garde des Consuls:

Most primary sources put the strength of the Consular Guard contingent at about 800 men. Furthermore, the official order of battle archived in the French Ministry of War lists the contingent as being both Grenadiers and Chasseurs of the Consular Guard, although sources often refer to them collectively as Grenadiers.

The Consular Guard had only recently been created; Bonaparte had decided to rename the Guard of the Directorate after his coup d'etat. In 1800, it was still a constitutional Guard of all three Consuls, although in practice it was only the First Consul who had real power in France. Nevertheless, the bulk of the Guard comprised veterans of the old Directorate Guard, particularly so in the Grenadiers. From surviving records, many of them had already served in the Guards for a significant part of their careers. Furthermore, these were men who had always been based in Paris. However, Bonaparte had plans to transform them into something very different; they would become a personal Guard, politically loyal to him. At Marengo, the Guard took part in perhaps the most iconic and misunderstood episode of the battle; its counterattack on Ott's Second Column.

By early afternoon, Ott's Column had captured Castel Ceriolo and was advancing south. The French had already tried to counterattack, without success. The Austrians now controlled the open plain to the north of the Tortona road. They now threatened to outflank and cut off the French line of retreat. The extent of Bonaparte's desperation at this point is measured by the fact that he was prepared to commit his last reserve to securing his northern flank; both his own Guard and his last three demi-brigades. In the fighting that followed, it was the Guard that advanced against the Austrian positions. The Austrian official military journal 'Osterreichische Militarische zeitschrift' published a report setting out the chain of events:

'The Garde Consulaire, formed up in column, crossed the plain and advanced against the forces of Fieldmarshal-Lieutenant Ott. This column employed a screen of sharpshooters that preceded it at a distance of sixty paces, covering its movement. Fieldmarshal-Lieutenant Ott took note and ordered the 10th Lobkowitz Dragoon regiment to charge against it. The enemy immediately closed ranks, deployed its 4 cannon, waited until the dragoons had broken into a gallop and then fired grapeshot, forcing them to retreat. A few squadrons of Champeaux's French dragoons, which supported the Garde, took up the pursuit of our cavalry and the Garde once again began its advance. General Gottesheim immediately advanced against this French cavalry with his Hungarian 51st Splenyi regiment, deployed in line. These enemy horsemen also retreated at the first cannon shots. However the 51st Splenyi regiment, supported by a battalion of the 28th Frohlich continued their advance against the Garde, and soon engaged in combat. The enemy also deployed and a rolling volley fire commenced, continuing for some time, with neither side gaining the upper hand. All of a sudden, Colonel Frimont arrived with 4 squadrons of hussars and charged directly into the rear of the Garde column, arriving at speed from the direction of Marengo. The Garde column collapsed and its men scattered. The soldiers of the Garde were nearly all either killed or captured and their cannons captured too. This brilliant action seemed to have decided the battle. It was about one o'clock.* The French now commenced a general retreat, offering only sporadic resistance, from then on. The Corps of Lieutenant-General Victor was now in complete rout.'
Osterreichische Militarische zeitschrift

In the end, the Guard was enveloped and overwhelmed by a combined Austrian infantry and cavalry attack. Several hundred Grenadiers surrendered although they did not remain prisoners for long. They were returned almost immediately after the battle as a prisoner exchange, in accordance with the treaty agreement.

136 The French Army of Reserve

Figure 38

137 The French Army of Reserve

Figure 40

Figure 39

138 The French Army of Reserve

Figure 41

Figure 42

Covering the Grenadiers as skirmishers, were the Chasseurs a pied of the Guard. In 1800, they were very different men to the tall Parisian-based Grenadiers. With an average age of 26 and average height of only 5ft7in, these men had been Bonaparte's personal bodyguard or 'Guides' and had only recently been incorporated into the Guard. * They were an elite within and elite; tough, hand-picked veterans of Egypt and the Italian campaigns, and personally loyal to Bonaparte. It was the Chasseurs who provided the screen of skirmishers. Austrian accounts state that the Grenadiers were supported by a battery of light artillery; two of these cannon belonged to the Guard Horse Artillery.

The uniform of the Guard is well documented in written and pictorial sources, including Hoffman, Potrelle and Poisson. The Grenadier in Figure 38 is based on all three sources, with the bearskin plate based on a surviving example at the Musee d'armee. The Grenadier coat had hardly changed since the days of the Directorate and would continue to remain unchanged throughout the Empire. It was based on the infantry coat but with small differences which included: red turn-backs, a blue collar, no lapel piping and white cuff flaps with red cuffs for Grenadiers. They were probably equipped as they were in the later consulate; with a knapsack, a good-quality blue greatcoat and a white and blue striped waxed-bag that contained an off-duty bicorn. Gold grenade badges adorned the turnbacks (facing outwards) as well as the cartridge case. NCOs had gold thread mixed into the red fabric of their epaulettes and sword knots. The back of the bearskin had a white over red cloth cross. Potrelle shows the Guard wearing a white raquette cord draped from lower right to upper left, a detail reproduced in this figure. Hoffman also shows, the white waistcoat as relatively long, reaching almost to the thighs for all Guardsmen, including Grenadiers.

Figure 40 represents a Chasseur of the Consular Guard as portrayed in prints by Hoffman and Poisson. Although they would have looked indistinguishable at a distance, there were marked differences in uniform between Grenadiers and Chasseurs. For the Chasseurs, the narrow coat lapels were cut like those of the light infantry and their sleeve cuffs were pointed, with two buttons but no cuff flap. Epaulettes were green, piped red; the plume was red over green. Badges on the coat's red turn-backs comprised a white grenade and a white hunting horn, as shown. The bearskin had no front plate, but Hoffman also depicts it as shorter than the Grenadier bearskin. A well-equipped unit like the Guards would almost certainly have worn white summer gaiters. Hoffman's prints show the Guard raquette cords as passing from upper right to lower left. Full dress uniform also included powdered hair, tied in a queue.**

Hoffman's prints also show Guard musicians including battalion drummers. The drummer in Figure 39 is based on this print. Unusual points to note include the red raquette cord; the red coat collar; the red and gold musicians' galloon ribbon and red epaulettes covering red and gold shoulder pads, known as 'swallows nests'.

The Sapper of the Consular Guard Chasseurs in Figure 41 is based on a print by Poisson. Poisson includes details which may relate to the Sapper's NCO status; these distinctions include a line of red piping to the forward edge of the coat collar; gold piping to the Chasseurs' green epaulettes as well as gold grenade badges and hunting horn badges. Other than this the uniform is very similar to that of the chasseur private, shown by Hoffman. Poisson's Sapper also carries what appears to be a tool pouch with brass badges that includes a crossed-axe design. His belt has a pouch to the left of the belt buckle which carries what might be a brass knife or bradawl. He is shown carrying a light hatchet.

Sappers appear to have been very much part of both Austrian and French armies throughout the 1790s and were well established by 1800. They marched at the head of any battalion column in both armies and carried NCO status. The inset image shows a sapper's bearskin, heavy siege-axe and chisel as portrayed by Langendijk on a sapper of the 53rd Demi-Brigade.

*Stutterheim puts the figure at 500 guard prisoners. Official Austrian sources state that the Guard was engaged and beaten shortly after 1pm, whilst French accounts state that this occurred over an hour later, between 2-3pm. This book takes the view that the timing given by General Victor of shortly after 2:30pm is more plausible. Austrian official journals wanted to emphasise that they had won the first stage of the battle early on, and this probably accounts of the disparity in timings.
**Cheap military hair powder was made from flour, chalk and grease. It hardened like plaster and offered some protection from lice, hard knocks and the elements.

Figure 42: Sergeant of Gendarmes: Gendarmerie: Army of Reserve

The mounted Gendarmes were an essential part of the Army of Reserve. They often acted as personal guards for Divisional Generals and a unit was present at Marengo, with Bonaparte's cavalry.

Louis XVI had a mounted military police corps, 5000 men strong, called the Marechaussee. With the advent of the revolution, this force quickly switched allegiance to the republican government. It was renamed the Gendarmerie and became part of France's internal security force, which also included the National Guard. However, the structure, equipment and uniform of the Marechausee remained essentially unchanged. In 1800, they still usually operated as small 6-

ман brigades. The Gendarmerie became essential to Napoleon's efforts to restore law and order within France, as well as organizational discipline within the army. In particular, he wanted to stem the desertion and banditry that plagued army lines of supply and communications. Under the consulate, the Gendarmerie were to triple in size, effectively becoming a separate army corps by 1804, with over 15,000 men.   The Gendarmerie of the early 1800s could include rough, gritty individuals, like the ones Jean Baptiste de Marbot met in 1802:

'The gendarmes belonged to the force at Peyrehorade and were returning to barracks after having eaten a good lunch at Orthez; they seemed somewhat drunk. The older of the two asked for my papers, so I handed him my passport; this stated that I was a Sous-Lieutenant in the 25th Chasseurs a cheval. He exclaimed, "You're no Sous-Lieutenant. You're too young to be an officer!" "But the passport description says I am not yet 20 and you can see it is completely in order."
"So what? You've forged it. The Chasseurs have a green uniform but your dolman is yellow, so I'm arresting you as a deserter."
"Very well but when we get to Orthez, I can prove that I am an officer and this passport is valid." My arrest didn't worry me much, until the gendarme declared that he was taking me to Peyrehorade instead. I replied that he had no right to do that. As I had a passport, regulations stated that he should accompany me to Orthez, but that he could only require me to return to Peyrehorade if I had no papers at all. The younger gendarme, who also appeared to be more sober, agreed with me and a lively argument began. The two horsemen began to openly insult each other and in the midst of torrential rain, drew their swords and came to blows. Afraid that I might get injured, I jumped into the ditch by the side of the road, sinking to my waist in water, before climbing out to the safety of the nearby field. From there I watched the fight. The gendarmes were only able to land light blows as their horses, frightened by the thunder, would not hold still and their heavy, sodden cloaks appeared to protect them. Suddenly the horse of the older gendarme stumbled and its rider fell in to the ditch, emerging covered in mud. He now also found that his saddle harness had broken. With no choice but to walk home, he told his companion to guard me.' I was left in the charge of the more reasonable gendarme who decided to let me go on my way.
Marbot

Figure 42 is based on another Hoffman print showing a consular gendarme. Hoffman shows the gendarme in a uniform very similar to that of the French Heavy-Cavalry, but with buff-coloured breeches and waistcoat. The saddlecloth is also shown as almost identical to that of the Heavy-Cavalry, though the rear corner has a white grenade badge in place of the Cavalry regimental number. The gendarme does not wear a cross-belt and cartridge pouch, though he would

have been armed with pistols kept in holsters at the front of the saddle. The gendarmes carried their own version of the straight-bladed An IV fleuron sword. The inset image has the standard An IV hilt, whilst the marechausee-gendarme version was adorned with a sun-burst decoration as shown. Officers of the gendarmes had similar coats but with white piping and more elaborate versions of the gendarme sword. Gendarmes were not merely given police duties. When called upon, they were also expected to fight as cavalry. Captain Aubry of the 12th Chasseurs was relieved to have one group of gendarmes join a charge:
'Throughout the battle, our three regiments remained under cannon fire. The Colonel had told me to cover these regiments, but as we had only infantry in front of us, we were exposed to cannon fire. Within a short time, I had lost half of my 48-man platoon, with either the horses or the men becoming casualties. At this point, I noticed that the enemy showed signs of retreating and sounded the charge. A dozen gendarmes had joined my platoon; all excellent cavalrymen on powerful horses. So, sabres drawn, we charged and reached the three enemy guns. The artillerymen had no muskets so we captured all three cannon, their caissons and their wagons within sight of our own troops.'
Aubry

Figure 43: The First Consul: Napoleon Bonaparte in the uniform of a 'General en Chef' of the French Consular Republic.

Napoleon Bonaparte was careful to cultivate his public image, but this image changed with the changing nature of his political power.

The image in 1800 was still that of a Commander in Chief of French armies of the new consular republic. As such, Napoleon still wore the uniform of a French republican general. Figure 43 is based on a whole series of formal contemporary paintings of Napoleon from 1795 to 1800. In fact, the uniform and equipment he wore at Marengo is still conserved and on display at the Musee d'Armee. Lejeune's painting in 1801 of the battle of Marengo is the first in which Napoleon is shown wearing his soon-to-be characteristic grey-brown overcoat. However, this is worn over a general's uniform.

The new 1798-pattern uniform was standard to all high-ranking French generals with few variations. It consisted of a dark blue double-breasted coat with a red stand-fall collar, trimmed with gold oak-leaf brocade. A red waistcoat and blue breeches were worn underneath. The general's bicorn was also trimmed in gold galloon with large tricolore 'panache' ostrich feathers. A tricolore sash was also worn usually covering the sword belt, though in this instance the belt is worn over the sash. The republican phrygian cap motif adorned the pommel of the general's sword and a classical victory trophy was embossed on the gilded buttons.   Differences in the uniform of generals is listed below, but in practice these were not followed, as even Generals like Lannes preferred tricolore feathers to the regulation red (for Divisional Generals).   General Lannes is described by his aide de camp, Antoine Nogues:

'Our skirmishers advanced and behind them, our columns of infantry followed closely.   General Lannes had advanced ahead of our skirmishers and was between them and those of the enemy.   There he was, in full brocaded uniform, galloon hat, adorned with large tricolore ostrich feathers, disdainful of enemy bullets; he said they were shooting over him, yet they nevertheless caused a number of deaths and casualties.   At that time, the old republican spirit still animated the best of our leaders.   The enemy retreated towards Castelnovo de Scrivia and we then entered Voghera.'
Nogues

Like Lannes, Bonaparte also modelled himself on the archetypal republican general; hero of the republic.   However, even in this early image, there was a gradual but significant change.   In 1795-6, paintings of Napoleon show him wearing the tricolore sash and plume, worn by every other General in every officially commissioned painting.   By 1800, paintings by artists like David or Andrea Appiani begin to discard these symbols of the French republic. Napoleon is shown bareheaded or wearing the bicorn without the plume.   Even in paintings where other generals are shown wearing tricolore symbols, Napoleon does not (as in Thevinin's Crossing of the St Bernard Pass painted in 1806-7).

How one dressed was important. In the period immediately after Marengo, political allegiances were reflected in how one chose to dress.   Opponents of Bonaparte like the group of officers who gravitated around General Moreau dressed in the austere spartan style of the Jacobins.   Napoleon however, expected his followers to show their loyalty by flouting this republican tradition.   General Thiebault found this out, to his cost when attending a function in Paris:

'Due to numerous delays we arrived just as the show was ending. Bonaparte was just exiting the area where the theatre had been staged and was entering the ballroom. I found myself in his path and as he passed me he stopped, turned and gave me one of the coldest looks I have ever seen.

You see, it had been the fashion until then to wear a clean, simple style of clothing; this simplicity was part of the accepted culture. Moreover, I don't like luxury and have never liked it. So, I had arrived at the ball dressed in a new uniform, but without brocade or adornments. But now Bonaparte, who maintained a very simple style of dress for himself, wanted to impose a new style of luxury on all those who surrounded him or who held government positions. Thus, his aides-de-camp, his ministers and almost all his generals covered

144   The French Army of Reserve

Figure 43

themselves with gold and brocade; this style of dress was further popularised by the vain way in which they conducted their political affairs. In the midst of all this stately pomp, my own uniform appeared, I admit, somewhat modest. Furthermore, the contrast it produced appeared to suggest a certain disdain for the ideas of the new First Consul and for the deference he demanded from his followers. From the day of that ball, he adopted a colder attitude towards me, bearing a grudge as only a true Corsican would.'
Thiebault

The First Consul continued to have a powerful group of potential enemies; these included republican sympathisers like General Moreau, commander of the Army of the Rhine. Given this situation, it is difficult to see how Bonaparte could have maintained his friendship with someone as outwardly republican as Desaix, had he lived. Yet Bonaparte was, and remained, a man of subtle contradictions. However, in June 1800, all this was yet to unfold. At Marengo, Napoleon was or acted the part of a citizen-general of the Consular Republic, leading a republican French army. To fully understand the battle, one must also understand something of the extraordinary qualities of the man who wore this uniform. Bonaparte's reaction to the destruction of the Consular Guard and the disintegration of his army, offers a vivid insight into his remarkable self-confidence. Guard Chasseur Krettley's memoirs record these moments, witnessed by him:

'Noticing that (they were in range of the road) the enemy commenced a harrowing artillery bombardment. Their cannon were now being loaded with solid shot. In this disastrous situation, we could find no cover. The First Consul appeared determined to improve our position, but it seemed to have now become far too perilous and difficult. Men fell all around him, but he did not even wince. He appeared to have his gaze constantly fixed on the enemy and was blind to everything else; he did not reply to his generals, who offered observations. After a while, the bombardment died off a little. At this, General Bessieres and General Duroc, seeing that their comments were having no effect, took the decision to seize him by the shoulders and drag him away from this exposed area, where he might be killed at any moment. As they were in the process of leaving, Bonaparte suddenly caught sight of Desaix who had just arrived, leading his division. At this he cried out, 'Victory is ours!'
Krettley

His reaction and behaviour at this critical moment in the battle is mentioned by nearly everyone who witnessed it. General Victor, who may have been closer than Krettley, claims that Bonaparte considered one final attack to stem the

Austrian advance or die trying. Yet Victor also says that Bonaparte did not, for one moment, betray his doubts:

'At this point, the situation was very critical indeed for Bonaparte. He knew that if the Austrians were to continue their success and claim a victory at the end of the day, this would cause irreparable damage to his glory, reputation and his bid for power. But no outward signs betrayed this hidden emotion. His features showed no hint of worry and remained impassive. His words were firm and sonorous. His eagle gaze surveyed this vast battlefield, covered with debris and corpses, with an assurance that seems to defy fortune and guarantee victory.'
Victor

Generals under the rank of Commander in Chief wore gold oak leaves on the collar, cuffs and pockets; in addition, they wore:

-General de Division: red ostrich feathers and tricolore plume with red sash fringed with the tricolore.
-General de Brigade: tricolore ostrich feathers and plume with blue sash fringed with the tricolore.

Figure 44: Gun Commander: Artillerie Legere: Garde des Consuls: General Bessieres: Battery supporting final French counterattack

The Consular Guard had a battery of Light Artillery with 6 guns. During the consulate, Light Artillery equated with Horse Artillery. Although Horse Artillery guns were often of lighter calibre, the Guard still had three 8-pounder cannon – large, effective battlefield guns. In the French Horse Artillery, all gunners rode horses, whilst the limbers were used exclusively to pull the guns. This made French Horse Artillery much faster than its Austrian counterpart.

By 6pm, the Guard Artillery had only three of their six guns left. They had set these up in battery, supporting the attack of the 9th Legere. The Gun Commanders serving them had a tremendous amount of discretion when it came to controlling their guns. When General Marmont ordered them to cease firing and move forward, the gunners ignored him and continued firing. Their judgment proved to be better than that of their General, and it contributed to the French victory. Marmont describes what happened in detail:

'I told Desaix I would set up a battery using the 5 guns that had survived the battle intact, to which I would add 5 more guns which had just arrived from the

147 The French Army of Reserve

Figure 44

Scrivia and a further 8 cannon belonging to his own division; this would give us a battery of 18 guns.

"That's good," replied Desaix, "Look, my dear Marmont, we want cannons, lots of cannons, and make the best use of them!"

The 18 guns were quickly set up as a battery, which occupied about half our front-line to the right of the Tortona road; our battery started slightly to the north of the road itself. Our sudden and intense bombardment caused some hesitation in the advancing enemy and halted their advance. Meanwhile, the Boudet division formed up, partly in assault-columns and partly in line. The First Consul rode along its lines and encouraged the men with his presence and with his words. After a 20 minute bombardment, the entire division began its advance. The infantry soon passed my battery, so I gave the order to follow the advance. I ordered the guns to be turned around, so that they could follow the infantry, but I had problems getting the gunners to do this. Despite my orders, they wanted to continue firing, aiming through the gaps between our infantry units. I finally made them do it, but had to order the gun teams to move, gun by gun. I had just arrived at the extreme left wing of the battery, just by the Tortona road, where 3 guns were busy firing. These guns included two 8-pounders and a howitzer, served by the gunners of the Consular Guard. I had to threaten these gunners in order to get them to follow my orders; and the horse teams, hooked to the drag-lines (prolonges), were about to begin to pull the guns around. Suddenly, I saw to my left and in front, the infantry of the 30th Line in flight and disorder. I immediately repositioned these 3 guns in battery and had them charged with grapeshot, and then waited.

Emerging from the smoke and dust, about 50 feet behind the fleeing soldiers of the 30th Line, I could make out a column in battle order. At first, I thought they were French, but then I recognised them as a large column of Austrian grenadiers. We had enough time to fire four rounds of grape-shot from each of our three guns, when Kellermann passed in front of my guns with his 400 cavalrymen. He charged and smashed into the side of the enemy column and the grenadiers were forced to lay down their arms. If the charge had been made three minutes later, our guns would have been taken or forced to retreat. If this had happened the enemy column might have been able to fire on our cavalry, having been given time to recover from our grape-shot. The same poor result might have happened if the charge had been three minutes earlier. It required this precise timing and combination of attack to produce a result that was so spectacularly successful and, I must admit, unexpected. Three thousand Austrian grenadiers were killed or taken prisoner, as well as General Zach, Chief of Staff and the true commander of their army... These events took place under my very eyes and only a few feet away from me. There has been much discussion about this part of the battle. But what I say is exactly what happened.'

Marmont

There are good reliable sources for the uniform of the Guard Artillery in the early consulate and Figure 44 is based on both Hoffman and Lejeune. It depicts a Guard uniform which, once again, was to change little throughout the Napoleonic period. Horse artillery were considered an elite, expected to be both cavalrymen and artillery gunners. As such, the gun commander has all the equipment of a light cavalryman including a sabre and horse furniture similar in pattern to that of the Guard Chasseurs. The uniform was based on a blue version of the light cavalry dolman and breeches, as shown. Lace and braid were aurore (red-orange) and braid was arranged in three columns of 14-16 rows. The barrel-sash in this period was aurore and yellow. There were no shoulder-straps or trefoil straps and buttons were brass. The consular sabretache was as shown; the officer's sabretache was trimmed in gold thread and is shown inset. An important point to note is that the artillery dolman during the consulate appeared to be smaller than that worn by the Chasseurs. As an NCO, the Gun Commander had a double raquette cord, with raquettes fixed on the right of the dolman and red plume on the left. In the later consulate, after 1801, the Guard artillery also began to wear a second uniform based on the cavalry habit coat.**

*At an earlier stage, the artillery of the Guard, or at least part of it, may have been uniformed in green pelisses, similar to those worn by the Chasseurs; Hoffman's prints includes one artillery officer dressed in this way.
**See Uniforms of Austerlitz – also in this series.

Figure 45: Gunner 'Ramrod' for 8-pounder: Artillerie a Cheval: 2nd Company of 2nd Horse Artillery Regiment: Supporting Watrin's Division on Northern flank

Figure 46: Gunner 'Firer' for 4-pounder: Artillerie a Cheval: 4th Company of 5th Horse Artillery Regiment: Attached to General Rivaud's Brigade, defending Marengo.

French artillery at Marengo was almost exclusively Horse Artillery. Horse Artillery Regiments were considered more mobile and better capable of crossing the St Bernard.

However, they were also the very best that French artillery had to offer. In 1800, no other foreign army had full horse artillery, including the Austrians. The French Horse-Artillery wasn't merely mobile; it was designed to attack aggressively with cannon, often in close co-operation with cavalry.

Gun-teams rode into battle on horseback and were dressed and armed like the cavalry they supported. Guns would be driven by fast 6-horse limbers and the whole Battery would keep pace with cavalry. Guns could be unlimbered and fired within a matter of seconds, usually at extremely close range, firing canister or grape shot. Canister or grape-shot rounds contained several hundred musket-sized pellets and the effect would be like an explosive burst of machine-gun fire.

However, at Marengo, the Horse Batteries were not used for the attacking role they had been designed for. The shortage of guns meant they were used to defend fixed positions, always outgunned and outnumbered by the opposing Austrian guns.

Each Battery-Company usually had 4 officers and about 100 artillerymen serving a battery of four guns and two howitzers. The guns were usually 4-pounders and 8-pounders. Within each Company would have been specialists like farriers, blacksmiths and trumpeters. The 2nd Company of the 2nd Horse Artillery regiment was mentioned in despatches for its brave conduct in supporting General Watrin's division on the northern flank. Its Captain Lechoux and 13 gunners were wounded with 3 killed. The 2nd Horse Artillery were also awarded three citations for exceptional bravery:

2e RÉGIMENT D'ARTILLERIE LÉGÈRE.
Sabre of honour awarded to Lt. CONRAD, second lieutenant in the company of the 2nd horse regiment. Distinguished himself throughout the battle and had a leg taken off by a cannon ball: "Return to your guns, and point a little lower," he said to the gunners who crowded around to help him.
Two grenades of honour to REINAL, gunner-aimer. —Dismounted an enemy gun and then seized it.
SANSGENE, Sergeant-Major— Acts of heroism.

The uniforms of the Horse-Artillery followed those of the French light-cavalry, and could be every bit as idiosyncratic. Artillery uniforms only became standardised under the consulate after 1801. Before 1800, Horse-Artillery often adopted the equipment of the cavalry units they were attached to, often through necessity. However, most Horse-Artillery uniforms followed that of the chasseurs a cheval, with one uniform based on the dolman and another based on the cavalry 'Habit' coat; both were used contemporaneously.

These artillerymen looked very different to the superbly equipped artillery batteries of the Grand Armee in 1805. Figure 45 is based on a watercolour by Lejeune, painted in the early consulate. The gunner is dressed in a long blue coat with lapels and blue cavalry riding-trousers. The coat has pointed cuffs with two buttons and red piping. He wears light-cavalry boots with fixed rounded spurs. He has a red and yellow barrel-sash covering a braided waistcoat or dolman. Red epaulettes are worn pushed back behind the shoulders. His 1786 pattern hussar sabre is suspended on a buff-coloured sword belt and his port-fire pouch cross-strap is also buff coloured. Perhaps most unusual of all, is the 'flamme' (or wing) which is wrapped around his head-dress. The flamme completely covers what is underneath, so it is impossible to determine whether it is a shako or mirliton. The flamme material is also covered in fine hairs suggesting it may be animal skin rather than fabric. A semi-circle of the same material is fixed at the front to form a peak. Wrapped around this head-dress and attached to buttoned loops, is a red raquette cord. The gunner's long hair is in cadenettes which are tied back to form a queue; in the style of the hussars.

The Horse artilleryman in Figure 46 is based on prints by Seele and another print in the Augsberg manuscript. He wears the same blue coat as in Figure 45, identical in every detail; his blue breeches have two knot-design braid decorations. Unusually, he wears an infantry-style striped double-breasted waistcoat and a dragoon helmet.

With peace in 1801 and Bonaparte's root and branch reorganisation, the Horse Artillery took on a more standardised uniform. The shako with flamme is the sort of equipment that was being introduced in 1800, but was by no means universally worn. It is shown on a series of drawings of consular Horse-Artillery made by Duplessis Bertaux.
The consular Horse-Artillery sabretache (hussar-satchel), saddle cloth and valise (cavalry knap-sack) were blue with a red border; the sabretache is shown by Suhr and Duplessis Bertaux as having a red regimental number on a blue background, circled by a green leaf garland; a red border runs along the outside edge. It must be assumed that this is the style of saddle cloth and horse furniture that was also used in 1800. Coignet describes how the guns of the Army of Reserve were carried over the Great St Bernard pass:

'Here we dismounted all the guns of our artillery in the presence of the First Consul. Each of the cannon was placed in a hollowed-out tree-trunk which served as a sledge, at one end of which was a hook to which we fixed dragropes. Each gun was commanded by a senior gunner (cannoneer) with 40 grenadiers under his command. We had to obey his every signal, observing absolute silence. If he said – halt – we stopped. If he said – advance – we did. He was boss. Next morning at dawn we were given biscuit and two pairs of shoes. I tied my large biscuits around my neck on a string. That evening the senior gunner organised the teams. Twenty would drag the cannon. The cannon was

152 The French Army of Reserve

Figure 45

153 The French Army of Reserve

Figure 46

fixed to ropes which were in turn fixed to ten short poles, acting like horse traces; two men pushed each pole. The other twenty men carried our muskets, knapsacks and equipment as well as the dismantled wheels and caisson for the cannon. The Consul had also employed local men from the mountains to transport other equipment left behind, paying them 6 francs and two days rations. Next morning our boss placed us in our trace-poles; I was in front to the right. This was the most dangerous position, right next to the precipice. Then we started. Two men carried each axle, two carried a wheel, four carried the upper part of the caisson, eight carried the chest and eight others the muskets. Every man had his role and his position. It was a terrible journey made in complete silence. Every now and then we halted and then marched on. The road passed up horrible slopes and along narrow paths. The road was covered with hard stones and ice which cut into our shoes. But this was nothing compared to what happened once we reached the snow; then things became very serious. The gun and sledge kept slipping towards the cliff-face and our gunner was often forced to realign it. Without his guidance and courage, we would have been lost… "Come on my horses," he would say, "Get to your positions and forward. Once we get past the snow we'll be better off. It won't be nearly as hard!"
Coignet

Coignet's description of an argument between this artilleryman and General Chambarlhac shows both the authority of cannoneers and the unique character of military discipline in the army of the republic:

Seeing our slow progress, General Chambarlhac came up to us wanting us to move more quickly. He strode up to the cannoneer and began to give him direct orders. "You don't command this gun. I've got sole command of it. These grenadiers are under my authority now, not yours. Go away!" When the General went forward as if to lay hands on him, the cannoneer shouted, "General, come any closer and I'll knock you down with my crowbar. Now get out of it or I'll throw you off the mountain!"
Coignet

Figure 47: Gunhandler serving howitzer: Foot Artillery: 5th Company of 1st Artillery Regiment: Supporting counterattacks of Monnier's Brigade and the Grenadiers of the Consular Guard

Figure 48: Officer of the Engineers: Attached to general Marmont's staff: Army of Reserve.

There were few Foot-Artillery units with the army at Marengo, although in theory every French line regiment in 1800 was supposed to have a battery of battalion guns. The only unit recorded in formal orders of battle being the 5th Battery Company of the 1st Artillery regiment. These men accompanied the counterattacks made by Monnier's Brigade (72nd, 70th demi-brigades and 19th Legere) and the Consular Guard infantry in the mid-afternoon. Victor claims this counterattack took place at about 2-3pm. Bonaparte scraped together all his remaining reserves of cannon, but could only provide these men with a single 8-pounder, a howitzer and two captured Piedmontese 6-pounders, to which he added two cannon from the Guard artillery. The last 4 guns were probably those identified by Austrian eyewitnesses as battalion guns supporting the Consular Guard.*

The French artillery in the late 1790s was perhaps the most advanced in the world. This was due to a series of long-term, far-sighted reforms, financed by the monarchy and inspired by General de Gribeauval, the Inspector of Royal Artillery. Guns were standardised as 4, 8 and 12 pounders. All equipment was standardised and produced to detailed models and templates. The principle for these templates was that each piece of a gun-carriage, limber or ammunition wagon (caisson) should be identical and therefore interchangeable, aiding repairs in the field. Gun-carriages were also made lighter, stronger and to a specific design. Small but important innovations included the use of poles to turn and aim guns, bricoles (rope and slings) to manually move guns forward, multi-use tools (like the ramrod-sponge) and a new gun-sight aiming system. All this was supported by a system of procuring raw materials – including timber-stocks that had been aged appropriately in order to build carriages. This system was to come to full fruition with the administrative and financial resources later provided under Bonaparte's consulate. Nevertheless, in 1800 Bonaparte had not been able to bring his artillery batteries across the Alps in significant numbers. He had gambled that he would be able to capture sufficient stocks of Austrian guns and ordnance in Italy, but this had not paid off. What guns he had captured were old decommissioned ordnance and unusable. At Marengo, this lack of artillery and ammunition nearly ended in disaster. A French War Department report summed up the situation:

156 The French Army of Reserve

Figure 47

Figure 48

The French passage of the Alps was astonishing in its audacity. However, this extraordinary enterprise had a far-reaching effect on the entire campaign. In particular, the supply problems it posed had not been carefully considered. For example, once in Italy, we had only been able to collect a small number of guns in good condition and very little ammunition. The 8 pieces found in Ivrea were in the worst condition; those taken from Pavia were almost all unusable; it was hardly possible to put 5 or 6 of them in good condition during the few days which elapsed between the capture of this town and the battle. The shortage of wagons offered no less difficulty; the French, who had advanced without any sort of train, found it very difficult to make up for it by commandeering wagons and carts from the countryside, as these were driven away at night or hidden from us.
War Department Report - Cugnac

The 1st Artillery regiment gunner in Figure 47 wears a uniform that was little changed from that of the pre-revolutionary Royal Artillery. The gunner is based on a Hoffman print of a gunner with tricolore cockade and other pictorial sources of the late 1790s including examples by Auguste, JF Dryander and Langendijk. The uniform of the Foot-Artillery was based on an entirely blue version of the standard infantry uniform, with artillery distinctions. For the gunners of the foot-artillery, this included blue facings for lapels, collars, shoulder straps, cuffs and cuff flaps, though Figure 47 has the red cuffs and cuff flaps shown by Auguste and Hoffman. These blue uniforms were always piped red, with red coat-tail turn-backs. Regulations prescribed blue facings for the artillery and black for the engineers, but sources show artillery gunners with very dark-blue (almost black) facings throughout this period.

After 1801, artillerymen appear to have had blue grenade badges on their coat-tail turn-backs, but not before 1800. Gaiters were black and are shown either long (above the knee) or short. Bicorns before 1800 usually carried red over black plumes – shown in several sources. On campaign, sources show the artillery wearing blue or dark coloured overall-trousers. Their right-shoulder cross-belts carried briquet short swords and their left-shoulder belt carried a Port-fire case (for cannoneers) or cartridge box (for supporting artillerymen); both appeared identical and both bore a brass crossed-cannon badge. Gunhandlers carried musketoons, as they were also expected to protect the guns when the need arose. They were usually equipped with the 1788 model fusil d'artillerie - artillery musketoon. With versions ranging from 120-130cm long, it was a more manageable weapon than the standard 152cm Charleville infantry musket or the longer dragoon musketoon (145cm long). These musketoons were also made from reconditioned muskets, where the end section of a damaged barrel would be removed, shortening the weapon; it was then finished with brass fittings. The Foot-Artillery played a much more important role in the defensive campaign fought by the Army of Italy along the coast. Sieges like Genoa were dominated by artillery duels, such as the one described by the 19 year old Marbot between the French artillery and British navy:

I have said the English only bombarded us at night. However, one day, when the English were celebrating some strange festival or other of theirs, their ships, adorned with flags, sailed up to the harbour in the middle of the day, and amused themselves by showering projectiles on us. The one battery which was in the best position to fire back, was near the harbour-mole, in a great tower-like bastion called the 'Lantern'. Massena ordered me to carry an order to the commander of this battery to take careful aim with all guns and to fire suddenly on an English brig which had arrogantly sailed up to the Lantern and anchored close to it. Our gunners fired so well that they hit the brig with a 500lb explosive shell, which smashed through its deck sinking it. The English Admiral ordered all his ships to fire on the Lantern which underwent an intense bombardment. My duty was to return to Massena, but what I saw held my attention. The firing platform of the Lantern was about the size of an average sized courtyard and armed with 12 very large cannon on huge carriages. It must have been a difficult target for the ships firing at us, but they nevertheless, managed to hit the Lantern with several shells. When these fell on the platform, all the gunners took cover under their carriages and I did the same. However, the explosive shells were unable to break through the thick flag-stones that paved the floor and ended up rolling on them, in unforeseeable directions. When they exploded, their fragments showered across the platform, flying beneath and behind the carriages. It was madness for anyone who was not under orders to be there, but I was gripped by a fearful exhilaration, almost joy, in being with the gunners and taking cover every time a shell fell and burst. This sport may well have cost me dear, for the deadly iron splinters caused carnage. Several gunners were severely wounded and one had both legs broken. One splinter cut straight through the timber of the caisson I was sheltering behind.
Marbot

Figure 48 is a Captain of the Engineers based on paintings by Langendijk, Lejeune and Dryander. Like all engineers, he wears black facings on his lapels, collar, cuffs and cuff-flaps although turn-backs are red like other artillery uniforms. Belts for officers of the engineers were black. Tricolore plumes and sashes were common features of the time, for all officers and like all junior officers he wears one full epaulette and one contre-epaulette. Qualifying for the engineers involved passing a series of very demanding exams and consequently its officers represented the technical and scientific elite of the artillery. Lejeune himself had only just qualified as an officer of engineers at the start of the 1800 campaign:

'I spent 15 hours a day studying for my professional exams and was encouraged and supported throughout by General Dejean of the Engineers, with whom I had campaigned in Holland. One day he called me over and said, "I'd like you to meet General Moreau. We're having lunch and I'd like you to be there."
At the lunch, while we were discussing the campaign in Germany, Dejean asked this famous Commander in Chief, "The Directorate treated you and the army so badly, so why did you not turn against them and drive them out?"
Moreau answered, "I did consider marching on Paris, seizing power and rescuing France; I would gladly have hanged all of them and all their supporters too. But I don't like conspiracy and it's not in my character."
Soon afterwards, the Minister of War summoned 40 officers to Paris who had been serving in the Engineers but had not yet graduated from the College of Mezieres. He had ordered us to be examined by a Commissioning Board, to ascertain whether we were of good enough calibre. I was very nervous about my exam date, as I have always been about exams. When the day arrived, I wore my uniform with black velvet facings worn by all officers of engineers, of which I was so proud. On the way to the exam, it poured with rain and the wind was making the shop signs sway back and forth. At that moment an ivy garland, the sign of Bacchus, was blown off the sign outside the wine-shop and fell at my feet. I picked it up, accepting it as an omen and augury and went on to await my exam. During the exam, the board set me some very difficult questions, challenging my answers in a hostile manner. The following day, I went to see the examiners and asked Abbe Bossut why they had treated me so harshly. He merely replied, "I wanted to be thorough, but you have nothing to complain about." A few days later, General Alexander Berthier, who I had never previously met, invited me to breakfast. At this meal, he told me that I was confirmed as an officer of the Engineers with the rank of Captain. He asked if I would also accept a post as aide-de-camp for the new Army of Reserve, which he was about to command.'
Lejeune

Lejeune accepted the post and soon found himself in Italy with the campaign in full swing, together with many of the other newly commissioned officers. One of his many missions included applying his engineering knowledge to the construction of pontoon bridges across the great Po river;

'After we captured Turin, one of my missions was the construction of boat bridges across the Po. I was to help oversee the work and return with a report to the General upon its completion. We had to collect the boats, rafts, timber,

ropes, anchors and other materials before construction even began. We worked for over 60 hours in pouring rain trying to build this bridge and finally finished at midnight on the 5th June.'
Lejeune

Other engineers were also employed in improving and maintaining the roads through the Alps. This was challenging work:

'The Consul arrived and immediately ordered heavy timbers to be delivered. He oversaw this in person, together with his engineers. First, they made holes in the rock of the cliff face. Then they fitted beams into these holes and laid planks on top of them. Crossbars and railings were also fitted. This bridge-like construction was completed in two days and all our supplies were then able to pass along it without further trouble.'
Coignet

*One of the 1st Regiment artillerymen, Gunner Renaud, was cited for bravery.

Figure 49: Artillery Train Driver: 1st Artillery Train battalion: Supporting cannon at Marengo.

Figure 50: Pontoneer Company: Attached to Engineers of Artillery Park: Torre Garofoli

The ability to cross the great rivers of the Po and its tributaries could mean the difference between success and failure in any Italian campaign. Napoleon had brought Pontoneers and Engineers with him, but he had no pontoon bridge equipment or the heavy wagons for transporting it. Nevertheless, his Pontoneers still proved their worth. They were able to construct 'pont volantes' or flying bridges; the next best thing. These were large-scale rafts tethered and propelled by a system of ropes and pulleys. Using these, his army had been able to cross the Po to the north and south of Piacenza, capturing the city and then repairing the boat-bridge already built by the Austrians. The men who built the flying bridges and repaired the captured boat bridges were the Pontoneers. They needed to be equally skilled at managing boats and bridging equipment as well as the horse drawn vehicles needed to transport or haul them into place.

'We set out in the morning and went towards the Po, which is a very large, deep river. Here we found a 'flying bridge' which could ferry 500 men in one journey. These men were hauled across on a platform, tethered to heavy ropes either side of the river. However, this took a lot of time, particularly when ferrying the

artillery. So it was very late when we reached the heights on the other bank. There amidst the desolation, we had to spend the night. From here, we marched on to Piacenza, a very beautiful city. Meanwhile, General Lannes was fighting the Austrians along the Po. Yet our division was merely sent from one place to another in an effort to assist our advance guard. We hadn't yet fired a shot. We only manoeuvred.'
Coignet

Figure 50 is based on a painting in the Zurich manuscript, datable to 1799-1800. The style of uniform is similar to other earlier pictorial sources showing French Pontoneers, including one in the Brussels Army Museum. The uniform was very similar to that of the Horse Artillery complete with blue Habit coat, waistcoat, breeches and light cavalry style boots. The manuscript shows red collars and red cuffs with three buttons and a looped braid design. Even more distinctive was the round hat with upturned brim. Similar in style to those worn by Austrian artillery, they appear to have had an anchor design in yellow braid under a tricolore cockade and red plume.*

Figure 49 shows a driver of the Artillery Train. The Artillery Train was a new service, which like the Pontoneers, managed both vehicles, complex ordnance and draught animals. The job of driving artillery limbers and ammunition caissons for the guns had traditionally been done by civilian contractors. However, these contractors had been unable and unwilling to cross the St Bernard. Far from being an organised crossing, Marmont's frantic letters to Bonaparte point to a crisis in his attempts to cross the Alps with artillery equipment:

'The peasants have all abandoned us; they've been put off by the harsh nature of this work. Even the muleteers are deserting us, dozens at a time. Our mules are dying of starvation. I had to employ a battalion of the 5th and about 600 men of the Loison division to pull the cannon and drive the wagons of the artillery. They have encountered excessive difficulty and made progress only under the blows of their officers. These men are now so exhausted, unhappy and low in morale that it is impossible to make further headway. No one could be expected to make this journey more than once. There is only one way we can do this. Order each division to drag its own artillery through the mountains. Also, send us as much rope as you can.'
Letter Marmont to Bonaparte 29th Floreal

The creation of the Train was in part a response to this crisis, but also an attempt to professionalize the support services for the army. Figure 49 shows the early uniform for this nascent branch of the army, based on prints by Langendijk,

162 The French Army of Reserve

Figure 49

Figure 50

Duplessis-Bertaux and Lejeune's 'Marengo'. The uniform was based on a light blue coat which could be either single breasted or with lapels, as shown. Collar, cuffs and turn-backs were red. Langendijk shows a rear pocket with three buttons, as in the inset. Headgear was a simple bicorn. Riding boots and cavalry side-buttoned riding trousers completed the uniform. The short artillery briquet (sometimes serrated) seems to have been standard equipment for the Train, even as early as 1800. All sources show elements of civilian clothing, including civilian waistcoats and neckties. At this early stage, many of the drivers would have been men who had previously worked for civilian contractors, but were now paid directly by the army. The men of the Train proved their worth at Marengo, with at least one documented instance of drivers saving abandoned guns.

In 1800 Black-Africans could be found in many parts of the French republican armies. Lejeune shows two in his painting of Marengo; an artillery train driver and an infantryman. At this stage, the French Consular Republic still supported and maintained relations with Toussaint L'Ouverture's Haitian Republic. Commerce and migration continued to flow between France and its former colonies. Haitians constituted a small but significant minority of the men under arms in the armies of the republic. Relations with the Haitian Republic would sour under Napoleon , with disastrous consequences both for Haiti and for the French invasion forces sent to conquer its people. Thiebault describes his memories of General Dumas, the Haitian-born father of Alexandre Dumas:

'Serving under Massena was a General de Division named Dumas, a mulatto. He was a very able man, and one of the strongest, bravest, most agile soldiers I have known. He had an extraordinary reputation in the Army. He had 20 citations for bravery, valour and achievement. On one occasion, we were only eight days in to our campaign, when he was attacked by Austrian cavalry while leading a unit of infantry. Riding a good horse, he could easily have retreated. Instead, he thought of his men and from the height of his horse helped them escape over a thick hedge, before charging and killing the first few approaching enemy cavalrymen. He only retreated when the main body of the enemy advanced. On another similar occasion, attacked by a superior force, he made sure that his troops could fall back, before being the last man to retreat, slowly and deliberately, even though under intense fire...However much he might be called the finest soldier in the French army and no matter how great his courage and ability, the colour of his skin proved his undoing. He was captured on his return from Egypt, thrown in a Neapolitan dungeon and poisoned by his jailers...he died of an ulcerated stomach. I was saddened by his death. I was close to him thanks to the friendship and consideration he showed me during the

campaigns we both served in. He is the only man of colour I have had the occasion to befriend.'
Thiebault

*This is a style of military hat which may also have been worn by some Legere units, as the Zurich manuscript also shows a chasseur from the 14th Legere wearing one. The description of the regulation 9th Legere uniform in 1800 also may be describing this very same style of roundhat (see above).

Figure 51: Trooper: 3rd Cavalerie de Bataille: Attached to Desaix's Division: Cavalry charge in final counterattack

Figure 52: Captain: 20th Cavalerie de Bataille: General Kellerman's Heavy Cavalry Brigade: Engaged throughout course of the battle.

The Cavalerie de Bataille were the Heavy Cavalry of the French republican and consular armies. It was not until 1804 that Napoleon added the cuirass and crested helmet to their equipment, transforming 12 cavalerie regiments into cuirassiers. There were four regiments at Marengo and their performance was exceptional.

Together with the four dragoon regiments and under the leadership of Generals Kellerman and Murat, they kept the Austrian cavalry at bay, effectively neutralizing the Austrian army's most powerful arm. Throughout the day, they maintained a localised superiority over the lighter Austrian dragoons who nearly always outnumbered them; in the centre of the battlefield, this numerical disparity was 3:1. The age of their leaders is also noteworthy; General Kellermann was 29 years old and Lieutenant-General Murat barely 33.

The designation of Heavy Cavalry was due less to the Cavalerie's equipment than to the size of the horses and the men who rode them. Most of the Austrian dragoon units were still equipped as light dragoons, riding horses no bigger than those used by hussars; the Cavalerie would have towered above them. This gave the Cavalerie a decisive advantage, as in their charge against Austrian dragoons who attempted to ford the Fontanone:

'Melas had ordered General Pilatti to take his dragoon brigade (1,300 strong) on to our left flank and to try to find a crossing there in order to outflank us. Pilatti's men found one possible crossing at a point where the Fontanone was covered by a small wood. One at a time, these dragoons managed to cross, so that several squadrons of the Kaiser Dragoons formed up on the other side of the ditch. But just as they were forming up in line outside the wood, Kellermann saw them and ordered the French 8th Dragoons to attack; these crashed into the Austrians, but soon had to retreat. Kellermann ordered them to the rear of his

heavy brigade which now advanced. The Heavy Cavalry advanced with swords drawn, slowly building up speed until, at fifty feet away, they broke into a full charge, throwing the Austrians back towards the ditch and beyond, forcing them to over-run their own infantry. More than 100 enemy cavalry fell into our hands and the rest were so badly beaten that they could not be deployed for the remainder of the battle.'
Victor

Kellerman's Heavy Brigade was made up of three regiments, the 2nd (120 men) and the 20th (300 men) and one squadron of 50 men from the 21st. These 470 men were supported by 1,300 dragoons from the 4 dragoon regiments present at the battle. Later in the day, during the French retreat, these regiments repeatedly charged and counter-charged pursuing Austrian cavalry, disrupting the enemy advance and shielding their retreating infantry.

By the time of the arrival of Desaix's reinforcements at about 6pm, Kellerman had only 150 men left including only 8 out of 28 officers; a 70% casualty rate. He was reinforced by 150 men from the 3rd Cavalerie and about 200 remaining dragoons. Kellerman's reply to Savary on being told to support Desaix's charge was blunt;

When the Aide-de-Camp Savary had conveyed to General Kellermann the orders of the First Consul, the General replied: "My men have been fighting since six o'clock in the morning. I have already made six charges, and have lost half of my men. The troops are completely exhausted: get us replaced by someone else.' Savary replied: 'You're the only ones left; the rest have disappeared or are too far off. You must go forward. Over there are the remnants of two dragoon regiments: attach them to your brigade.' Kellermann admitted the urgency of the situation, agreed to attack, and made his arrangements accordingly."
Savary

Despite the exhaustion of his men and horses, Kellerman's charge was spectacularly successful. It overwhelmed the Austrian Grenadiers, capturing some several thousand prisoners and initiated an Austrian retreat that quickly degenerated into a rout.

Figure 51 and 52 are both based on Hoffman's detailed paintings of the officers and men of the Cavalerie. The uniform of the French Cavalerie was based on a blue version of the cavalry Habit-Long with white pewter buttons. Facings were usually on the collar, cuffs, cuff-flaps, lapels and turn-backs. The facings of the

Figure 51

167 The French Army of Reserve

Figure 52

Cavalerie regiments at Marengo were either red or pink.* Legwear included doeskin breeches and tall heavy riding boots reaching to above the knee. A heavy straight bladed An IV sword was the main armament and troopers may also have been armed with pistols. Horse furniture was similar to that used later by the Cuirassiers with a half saddle cloth (demi-shabraque) and sheepskin trimmed in the facing colour: with the sole difference being the round valise of the Cavalerie. Bicorns were smaller and shorter than those worn by the infantry. They were adorned by a red over dark green plume. Only one Cavalerie regiment wore the cuirass; this was the 8th Cavalerie who were not part of the Army of Reserve and did not participate in the Italian campaign of 1800.

Officers wore epaulettes with metallic silver thread; braid and grenade badges were in the same metallic colour. Senior officers also wore silver-plated buttons. Officers also had their own version of the An IV sword with decorative hilt. The red over dark green plume was also wider and larger for officers. Officers' horse furniture included silver thread trim and double or triple cloth holster covers which replaced the sheepskin of troopers.

Within a year of Marengo, Napoleon began a process to equip the first 12 Cavalerie regiments with cuirasses and convert them into Cuirassier cavalry; a process which was still not wholly complete even in 1805.

Cavalerie Uniforms at Marengo

2nd	Scarlet lapels, turnbacks and cuffs; blue collar and cuff-flaps
20th	Pink lapels, turnbacks and cuffs; blue collar and cuff-flaps
22nd	Pink lapels, turnbacks, cuffs and cuff-flaps and collar
3rd	Scarlet lapels, turnbacks and cuff-flaps and collar; blue cuffs

Facings for other regiments included red for regiments 1-6, yellow for 7-12, crimson for 13-18, pink for 19-24 and orange for 25-29. Blue collars and cuff flaps for regiments numbered 2,5,8,11,14,17,20 and 23. Blue cuffs for regiments 3,6,9,12,15,18,21,24.

Figure 53: Trooper: 8th Dragoons: General Champeaux's Dragoon Brigade: Engaged throughout the course of the battle.

Figure 54: Trooper: 6th Dragoons: General Duvignau's Dragoon Brigade: Engaged throughout the course of the battle.

By far the largest contingent of French cavalry were the Dragoons, about 1,300 strong and comprised of four regiments; the 6th, the 8th, the 9th and the 1st Dragoons. The 8th, 9th and 1st appear to have been part of General Champeaux's Dragoon Brigade, operating in the centre and north of the battlefield. The 300 men of the 6th Dragoons in General Duvignau's light-brigade had bivouacked in Marengo itself overnight and would have been involved in the battle from the very start. It is probable they continued to provide close support to the courtyard of Marengo itself. However, there may never have been fixed positions in what rapidly became a confused and fast-moving battle.

'Our retreat from Marengo was executed in echelon starting from the left flank, which had suffered most in the battle. Each battalion retreating in order of closed columns. As soon as the Austrians realised our movement to the rear, they attacked with all their cavalry, which charged us and tried to cut us off. Their infantry also advanced in order of battle, formed in two lines and preceded by their 80 or so cannon which showered our ranks with grapeshot and explosive shells.
For their part, our men carried out this retreat with admirable professionalism. From time to time, they stopped, about-turned, fired volleys and waited for the smoke to lift in order to gauge the effect of their fire. They then turned again and continued their retreat at walking pace, whilst recharging their weapons. They were, I admit, wonderfully supported by our (dragoon) cavalry and by Kellermann's Heavy Brigade which covered our left flank. These dragoons retired by platoons at a trot, and from time to time turned to face the enemy, thereby countering their cavalry. By these manoeuvres, they were able to keep the enemy cavalry at a distance and prevent them from pressing too hard on our infantry. The dragoons gave our infantry time to reorganise when their columns lost formation and they prevented the enemy from taking any prisoners. On our right the dragoons of the Champeaux Brigade carried out a similar role, even though their brave leader had already been killed.'
Victor

Throughout the battle, the Dragoon units were used as a first line of cavalry reserve, counter-charging and covering retreating French battalion columns, as and when required; with the Heavy Brigade kept back as a strategic reserve. The charge against General Pilatti's Austrian dragoons is a case in point, with the 8th Dragoon regiment charging first, followed by the Heavy Cavalerie Brigade.

170 The French Army of Reserve

Figure 53

171   The French Army of Reserve

Figure 54

Dragoons were the general, all-purpose cavalry of all European armies. Yet French dragoons appear to have been equipped with larger, heavier horses than most of their Austrian counterparts. This characteristic continued under the consulate, when many Cavalerie regiments were converted to dragoons.
The basic dragoon uniform was based on the green Habit-Long, similar in many respects to the coat worn by the French infantry. Each of the 30 dragoon regiments had different coloured facings or arrangements of facings; facing colours could appear on the lapels, collar, turn-backs, cuffs and cuff flaps. The facing colours for the regiments at Marengo are set out below. Waistcoats were always white. Troopers wore doe-skin breeches and long riding boots fixed to the breeches by a buttoned strap. Green riding trousers were often worn over the breeches. These had leather reinforcement on the inner leg and a buttoned outer seam in the facing colour.

The 'classical' or 'Roman' helmet is the detail most closely associated with the dragoon uniform. It was a round brass helmet, completely round at the rear with no neck guard. The front peak was leather, though helmets of the period are often shown without this peak. The brass crest, rivetted to the helmet, had various decorative patterns; a black horsehair crest could be fixed to a tube at the front of the crest. The helmet was further adorned (and protected) by a brown fur turban or often by scaled-metal straps. Leopard-skin turbans were worn by officers.

Figure 54 is based on one of three detailed studies of dragoons painted by Lejeune in this period. Points to note are the strap-on spurs which could be removed when on foot duty. The dragoon also wears the sword belt extended and over his right shoulder, thus keeping the scabbard higher above the ground; something that was done for dismounted duties. His weapon is not the standard straight bladed An IV sword used by the Heavy cavalry, but a light 1790 Montmorency sabre with a shorter 80cm blade. All of the dragoons depicted by Lejeune are equipped with this sword; a light cavalry weapon also used by Chasseurs. The detachable peak is made from a very flexible strip of leather and was often not worn. Few of the dragoon helmets of this period show the fur turban prevalent in later years. Instead, helmets were reinforced with bands of brass scales; possibly detached metal chin straps tied around the helmet base. This is a detail found in other contemporary depictions, including Hoffman and Hauk. The trooper wears a long queue, bound in black cloth; his fatigue cap is rolled and fixed to the top of his cartridge pouch. The inset image shows the front of the dragoon helmet, worn by an NCO and distinguished by a blue tuft.

Figure 53 is based on a range of contemporary sources including Lejeune, the Augsberger prints, the Zurich prints, Hoffman and surviving uniforms from the Musee d'armee. The troopers of the 8th dragoons appear to have been supporting Kellermann's Heavy Brigade. This trooper wears the more standard 95cm bladed An IV sword, still decorated with republican 'fasces' and phyrgian cap symbols on the hilt and pommel. A bayonet frog could be attached to the belt. The bayonet was used for the dragoon musketoon which was carried on the right of the saddle in a sling. This 140-145cm musketoon was a shorter version of the 1777 Charleville infantry musket. The dragoon wears an additional belt over the left shoulder for his carbine clip, to which the musketoon was often fixed. The horse furniture follows that shown in the Zurich prints and by Lejeune which show other-ranks cavalry with full saddle cloths and round valises, covered by a folded red-white portmanteaux. Other dragoon regiments may well have been equipped with the half saddle cloths (demi-shabraques) and the square valises of later years, but there is little evidence of this before 1801. The Battle Honours awarded to the 1st, 6th and 9th Dragoons give an insight in to the type of fighting they were involved in:

Awarded to the 1st Regiment of Dragoons.— 2 carbines of honour.
BERGER, sergeant.— *In the first charge, near La Bormida, he broke through an enemy squadron formed in line, killed an officer who was at the head and then two light horse troopers.*
DECHAMET, dragoon.— *After having received a wound, he had retired to be dressed, when he saw his platoon under enemy attack; he returned through the musketry, assisted in rallying his comrades and remained with them until the end of the battle, although he lost much blood.*
Awarded to the 6th Regiment of Dragoons.— 2 carbines of honour.
CHAUVEAU, dragoon. — *Took a caisson and then recaptured it.*
CARPENTIER, dragoon. — *Was instrumental in the capture of about thirty prisoners.*
Awarded to the 9th Regiment of Dragoons.— 3 carbines of honour.
ISNARD, chief quartermaster. — *Charged an enemy platoon several times, killing an officer, and only withdrew after the end of the battle, though seriously wounded.*
JOUSSE, dragoon. — *Captured an enemy flag.*
JOBEY, dragoon. — *Killed two enemy troops, saved one of his comrades, and captured two enemy officers who had offered their purses to be set free, which he refused.*

Dragoon Uniforms at Marengo

Facing colours adorned the lapels and turnbacks of all regiments. In addition:

1st	Scarlet Facings	cuffs and cuff-flaps and collar.	(horizontal pockets)
8th	Crimson Facings	cuffs	(horizontal pockets)
9th	Crimson Facings	cuff-flaps and collar	(horizontal pockets)
6th	Scarlet Facings	cuff-flaps and collar	(vertical pockets)

Figure 55

175 The French Army of Reserve

Figure 56

Figure 55 and 56: Troopers: Grenadiers a cheval: Garde des Consuls: Present on the battlefield from mid-afternoon and committed to the final pursuit of routed Austrian cavalry, in the closing stages of the battle.

Although lacking in resources and ordnance, the Army of Reserve had a strong contingent of Heavy Cavalry, unusual for armies in the Italian theatre. The most prestigious of these heavy regiments were the Grenadiers a Cheval of the Consular Guard, probably about 200 strong. Although individually veterans of proven ability, the regiment itself had always been based in Paris, like the rest of the Guard. Napoleon was to turn it into something with a far more significant battlefield presence.

The Horse Grenadier Regiment arrived late in the afternoon on the day of the battle, accompanying Bonaparte from Torre Garofoli. Bonaparte tried to keep it as a reserve until the very end of the battle. Indeed, Bessiere's refusal to commit it to a full-scale charge earned him the opprobrium of army Generals like Lannes.

'The Consul now sent the Horse Grenadiers and Chasseurs of the Guard to support the army. We moved along the entire front, according to need, sometimes to the left flank, and sometimes to the right. At one point, General Lannes pressed us to make a charge, which did not have a successful outcome. At the time, he was being pursued by two enemy battalions with two cannon and a mass of cavalry behind them. His own troops were by now retiring in considerable disorder and he wanted to give them time to breathe and reorganise, so he ordered Bessieres to charge the enemy columns. The ground was not favourable, as it was covered with vines and obstructions. Nevertheless, we passed through the vineyards and arrived within range of the enemy infantry who were formed up in closed ranks, ready to fire. Colonel Bessieres was on the point of ordering a charge when the enemy's cavalry rode up and attempted to outflank us on our left flank. Bessieres ordered us to turn and face this new threat, which we did under fire from grapeshot and musket-fire. We then retired. General Lannes was very dissatisfied with our actions, complaining bitterly that we had failed to execute orders. However, I am certain that if we had executed his orders, very few of us would have returned alive.'
Eugene Beauharnais

Bessieres may have been under orders from Bonaparte to keep the Horse Guards out of costly engagements. However, the majority of cavalry action during the retreat consisted in manoeuvre and counter-manoeuvre; full-scale charges were always costly and hazardous. Facing off the enemy and preventing outflanking moves which could cut off and isolate retreating units was much more cost effective. Bonaparte finally committed his Horse Grenadiers only at the very end of the battle, as part of a general advance. As dusk approached, the Horse Grenadiers joined in with a final charge on the screen of Austrian rearguard cavalry, on the outskirts of Marengo.

'As night fell, the enemy were in complete disorder. Cavalry, infantry and artillery all converged in a mass towards the main road in the centre of the battlefield. We could see men being pushed off the bridge and falling into the water. The enemy had tried to withdraw their artillery first to prevent it being captured, but this now blocked the road. Murat, seeing the importance of increasing the enemy's confusion and further disordering them, ordered us to advance at full trot. Before long, we overtook a mass of infantry who were forced to surrender, having no further means of defence. In this advance, about 200 men of the Horse Grenadiers and Chasseurs of the Guard kept to the right of the road. On the left of the road were about 400-500 men of the 1st, 6th and 8th Dragoons and the 20th Cavalerie. Murat rode along our line throughout. Now, the decisive moment was upon us. Colonel Bessieres, inspired by the same ardour of battle which seized every one of us, sounded the charge, aiming at the exhausted mass of enemy infantry.
The enemy cavalry tried to intercept us, in an effort the shield the army. Their rapid pace, forced us to let loose our reins. The Horse Guards charged to the left, veering towards this enemy cavalry. About thirty feet in front was a drainage ditch which was all that separated us. Within 5 minutes we had crossed this, surrounded the first two enemy platoons and engaged. Overwhelmed by this charge and by the height of our horses and our men in their tall bearskins, the Austrian dragoons could not defend themselves. They were either cut down or put to flight. We took no prisoners, nor did we stop to capture horses. Our French dragoons also attacked the enemy from the right, adding to the carnage.'
Petit

Figure 55 is based on three sources showing Horse Grenadiers from the period; Hoffman, Lejeune and Rugendas. All show a remarkable consistency in uniform from the early consulate through to the Empire. The Grenadiers all rode black or dark horses. Even at this stage, the Grenadiers had two main uniforms, full dress and campaign dress. Lejeune has three Horse Grenadiers in his painting of Marengo and all wear the campaign dress surtout shown in Figure 56. Figure 55 shows the full-dress uniform, depicted by Hoffman. It was based on a blue long-tailed coat with white lapels, red cuffs with white cuff-flaps. Even at this early stage, details like the aurore (orange-red) braid aiguilette and red turnbacks with aurore grenades were fixed features in the uniform. Boots, breeches and waistcoat were similar to those of the Cavalerie. The cold-weather cape is shown as dark blue for officers and off-white for other ranks. Belts were completely white. Differences in this early version of the uniform include; the aurore piping on the collar; the aurore braid shoulder straps (which were later replaced with trefoils); and the very wide red plume. The bearskin was relatively short, similar in dimensions to that worn by the Chasseurs-a-pied. Hoffman shows the bearskin raquette and cord to be red, not aurore. Furthermore, the cartridge pouch had a single brass grenade badge and all brass buttons bore the republican fasces, as shown.

The saddlecloth and pistol holster covers had a double aurore border. However, two small differences to later years include a wider saddlecloth aurore border and a cylindrical valise. The Horse Guards were still armed with a full-length Guard's musket, complete with brass fittings, later to be replaced by a shorter dragoon-style musketoon. They had their own version of the An IV sword, with a triple bar hilt; officers had a hilt similar to the Cavalerie officer sword-hilt (see above). Officers wore gold-thread epaulettes and gold braid, galloon and piping instead of aurore.

Far from being esteemed as a prestigious unit, the Guard were shunned and disdained because of their links with Bonaparte. Elie Krettley describes a spate of duels and fights between republican sympathisers and Horse Guards in Paris soon after Bonaparte's coup d'etat. He describes how groups of cavalrymen from other regiments would intentionally pick quarrels and fight duels with Guard Chasseurs, often ending in large-scale brawls. His memoires point to the latent opposition to Bonaparte in 1800 and the very real weakness of his position within France prior to Marengo.

'If I mention these shameful incidents, it is to give the reader an idea of the political tensions at that time. These trouble-makers aimed at nothing less than to totally undermine the unity of the army...Harsh words were spoken and you can imagine, we were not men to take an insult. They called us Bon-a-pendre, a play on Bonaparte, which means good-for hanging and so the duels began... Two days after a large-scale brawl outside our barracks, we received a challenge to turn up at the Champs de Mars. We were outraged at the insolent messages sent to us on a daily basis and ignoring the express orders of our senior officers, we went to the rendezvous. We had hardly arrived, when a large crowd of soldiers and swordsmen moved towards us. Counting the men on either side, there were about 150 men armed with sabres and a pitched battle soon ensued.'
Krettley

Krettley says these tensions continued until the Guard were finally ordered to leave Paris and join the Army of Reserve.

Figure 57: Trooper: Chasseurs-a-cheval: Garde des Consuls: Engaged throughout the course of the afternoon.

Figure 58: Escort of the First Consul: Chasseurs-a-cheval: Garde des Consuls.

There were only about 150 Guard Chasseurs at Marengo and Figures 57 and 58 serve to show their uniforms and their recent history. The Guard Chasseurs were created when Napoleon incorporated his own squadron of personal bodyguards or 'guides' into the new Consular Guard in 1799. Most French Commanding Generals had a bodyguard of 'guides' and Bonaparte had created his own Guides in the 1796 Italian campaign. Antoines Nogues, an aide to Lannes, mentions their incorporation into the new Consular Guard:

'In Paris, Bonaparte was aware of a numerous throng of enemies, of all political persuasions, buzzing around him. It was then that Lannes received an order to form a new Garde des Consuls. The Garde comprised a regiment of Grenadiers and another of Chasseurs together with six squadrons of Grenadiers a Cheval and a Company of Guides, in which the young Eugene de Beauharnais was a sous-lieutenant; it also had several companies of Horse-Artillery and Foot-Artillery. Bonaparte held many parades and inspections with his new Garde and with the various army units based in and around Paris.'
Nogues

When the Guides became the Chasseurs of the Guard, they adopted a new hussar style uniform but retained their old uniform of the Guides, as an undress uniform. When platoons of the Chasseurs were chosen to escort the First Consul, they wore the old Guide uniform. Indeed, Bonaparte insisted on this, often wearing the Guide Habit coat himself as a measure against assassination. It is difficult to say which uniform was worn at Marengo, though Lejeune shows the Emperor escorted by two Chasseurs dressed in the Habit-coat of the Guides. In all probability, both uniforms were worn, depending on the orders of the day for each platoon.

An insight into the experience of the Chasseurs during the battle can be found in the memoires of the 18 year-old Eugene Beauharnais and of the much humbler but equally young trumpeter, Elie Krettley. The Chasseurs arrived on the battlefield as the retreat was in full swing:

'My Chasseurs were given orders to destroy any abandoned ammunition caissons and we undertook this mission with great intrepidity. We waited until the enemy

Figure 57

181 The French Army of Reserve

Figure 58

were almost upon us before setting fire to the caissons and then jumping on horseback to ride away, leaving the caissons to explode.'
Eugene Beauharnais

Other Chasseurs were given duties as and when they arose. Krettley was ordered to accompany an aide delivering orders on the front-line.

'During this great battle, I was on picket duty with General Bonaparte. At one point, he sent me to accompany an aide-de-camp to reconnoitre an advance made by the Bussi Dragoons on our left flank. I advanced quite close to this unit and an officer of theirs rode towards me to dispute my passage. I accepted the challenge which did not last long, as I killed him in less than a second and took his horse. We had almost made it to the French 8th Dragoon regiment, when a shell burst a mere ten paces from us, showering and blinding us with mud and dirt. Recovering from the explosion, we finally reached the Colonel (Millet) of the 8th Dragoons, delivering our orders. He immediately put his regiment in to action.'
Krettley

Later, Krettley was involved in charging Austrian cannon that had been firing directly at the French General Staff on the main road:

I put myself at the head of my small troop of 20 chasseurs (half the personal guard of the First Consul) and waited until the Foot Guides had gained a position on the flank of the enemy cannon. When they began to fire on the cannon, I judged it the right moment to act: "Comrades," I cried, "courage! Charge in open ranks".
I was well supported and the attack was so well executed that within 5 minutes the guns were ours. This action gained the thanks of the Consul and I was awarded a Trumpet of Honour.
Krettley

Hoffman painted a series of Chasseur uniforms, including both the Hussar-style uniform (Fig 57) and the Habit-coat (Fig.58). Figure 57 shows the full-dress uniform for the Chasseurs in the early consulate, based on Hoffman. It comprised the characteristic green dolman and red pelisse that the chasseurs were to keep for the next 14 years. However, there were important differences in this uniform worn during the early consulate. In 1800, the cloth breeches were red for both officers and men, with a knot design as shown. The consular sabretache is based on Hoffman and matches a surviving example in the Musee d'armee. The colpack had a very tall green plume with red tip and the aurore colpack cord ended in a tassel (without raquettes) below the tricolore cockade. Horse furniture included two brass star-burst disks and unusual straight brass and steel bridle bits. All braid and galloon was in the red-orange colour called 'aurore'; although for officers, aurore was replaced by gold. It is in this exact uniform that Charles Thevinin shows the Chasseurs crossing the St Bernard pass in his officially commissioned painting; completed in 1807.

The Guides' uniform in Figure 57 is not only shown by Lejeune but in another contemporary painting by Lussigny of a Chasseur in the Italian campaign, dated March 1799. Both depictions of this uniform are identical in every detail with the exception that Lussigny's figure wears a Chasseur bicorn with red plume and two aurore ties. The Guide uniform, based on the green Habit-coat and green breeches, changed little throughout the following decade. However, the early uniform also had important minor details not present in later versions of the uniform. These include; the braided trefoil shoulder straps; the aurore chevrons on the breeches; the 6 vertical button pockets on each coat-tail. Furthermore, the 1800 'colpack' depicted by Lejeune and Hoffman appears to have been much smaller than in later years, with a rounded top, similar to the early Foot-chasseur bearskin also depicted by Hoffman (see Fig 40 above). Indeed, the Foot and Horse Guides may originally have worn the same headgear, which they continued to wear when they both became Guard Chasseurs; headgear that was gradually replaced by new issue bearskins and colpacks. Senior officers in this uniform are shown wearing their gold-thread aiguilettes on the right shoulder – the opposite side to troops. For officers, an ornate officers' saddle-cloth replaced the standard campaign sheepskin used by troops.

The inset images on both figures show two weapons, which appear to have been made especially for the Guard Chasseurs. The first was the Guard Chasseur sabre, modelled on the standard Hussar sabre but with brass hilt and scabbard. The second weapon was the 1793 short-muzzled cavalry rifle, produced at Versailles. There was a longer infantry version of this rifle (1.2m long); both were used by the Guard, though not exclusively. Two examples are on show at the Musee d'armee.

Towards the end of the battle, the Chasseurs joined in the general advance. Eugene Beauharnais describes this action:

'Finally, at about five o'clock, General Desaix reinforced us and the First Consul was able to resume the offensive. The troops of General Lannes, encouraged by this reinforcement, reformed and joined the advance upon an enemy that was now in retreat... Towards evening the Guard cavalry carried out an important charge.

The ground we crossed was difficult, as there were drainage ditches in our path, but we nonetheless charged a column of enemy cavalry, superior to us in numbers, just as it was forming. We pursued them as far as the bridge over the Bormida, fighting all the way.* The melee lasted 10 minutes and I considered myself fortunate to have escaped with only two sabre cuts to my saddle bag. On account of this, the following day, the First Consul promoted me to chef d'escadron. My Company of Chasseurs suffered many casualties, as of the 115 men we had at the start of the battle, there remained only 45 at the end. However, a picket of 15 chasseurs had guarded the Consul throughout and over the following day chasseurs who had been only slightly wounded or dismounted rejoined the ranks.'
Memoires du Prince Eugene

Unlike many other units, the Guard were able to return directly to Paris after the battle. They returned with Bonaparte, who was eager to use the victory to consolidate his political control. Eugene continues by describing the Guard's triumphant return, still clothed in the dust of battle:

'Then to the Champs de Mars, where a big celebratory parade was taking place. Here the troops of the Guard who had remained in barracks, clean and immaculately dressed, offered a striking contrast to those of us now returning from the Italian campaign, thin and exhausted and covered in dirt. However, the battle-worn appearance of our brave men only increased the enthusiasm and cheering of the Parisians. We did a circuit of the entire Champs de Mars to the roaring adulation and applause of the crowds that packed the surrounding slopes. It was one of the most beautiful moments of my life.'
Memoires du Prince Eugene

*Eugene Beauharnais must be referring to the bridge over the Fontanone, which he may easily have mistaken for the Bormida bridge with the approaching dusk. The Guard did not cross the Fontanone on the evening of the battle.

Figure 59: Trooper: 21st Chasseurs-a-cheval: Brigaded with the 12th Hussars and positioned north of Castel Ceriolo.

Figure 60: Trooper: 12th Chasseurs-a-cheval: Positioned 8km south of the battlefield. Attacked and pursued by the 7th and 9th Austrian Hussars

Both regiments of Chasseurs present at Marengo had been quartered several kilometres to the north and south of the battlefield, guarding the extreme flanks of the French army. Their distance from the battlefield is a measure of how little Bonaparte expected an attack at Marengo itself. Both regiments had a minimal direct impact on the battle, yet their presence on the flanks of the Austrian army certainly offset the Austrian effort on Marengo. This was particularly true in the south, where the men of the 12th Chasseurs appear to have kept over 2,000 Austrian Hussars out of the battle. However, the presence of the 21st Chasseurs in the north also tied down at least part of Second Column.

The 21st Chasseurs (about 360 strong) were brigaded with the 12th Hussars in the vicinity of Sale, about 15 km north east of Marengo. At the start of the battle, their commanding officer General Jean Rivaud (a relative of Olivier Rivaud, the General commanding at Marengo courtyard) began a cautious approach towards Castel Ceriolo. On approaching the village, his forward units came under fire from the much larger infantry and cavalry units of the Austrian Second Column; consequently, his brigade did not manage to reach the battlefield. Towards the close of day, when it became clear that the Austrians were in retreat, the 21st Chasseurs and 12th Hussars charged the rear-guard of Austrian cavalry, harrying the retreating Second Column troops as they moved through Castel Ceriolo. Despite their minimal participation in the battle, the presence of these Chasseurs caused concern to Ott's staff and may have contributed to their over-cautious advance.

The experience of the 300 men of the 12th Chasseurs at Castellazo to the south of the battlefield was very different. They were attacked and over-run by a large detachment of the 7th and 9th Austrian Hussars, commanded by General Nimbsch. This large column of 2,300 Austrian hussars had been sent away from the battlefield earlier in the day on the basis of erroneous reports of approaching French reinforcements. Whether they mistook the 12th Chasseurs for these reinforcements or not, they attacked, pursued and captured about two thirds of the regiment. Despite these losses, Bonaparte was pleased with the contribution of the 12th Chasseurs:

'Our regiment suffered severe losses at Marengo. We had been detached from the main army to cover the far left-wing of our position, but were attacked by a large force of enemy cavalry. In spite of our fighting reputation, many of our men were captured. Our Colonel Defrance was obliged to report in person to the first Consul the following day and he feared a severe reprimand. On the contrary, to his surprise, Bonaparte gave him a magnificent reception. He complimented and congratulated him on the services rendered by the 12th chasseurs in tying down a superior force of enemy cavalry. Had these enemy hussars not been engaged by us, they might have returned to the battlefield and changed the outcome of the battle itself.'
Souvenirs de Captaine Aubry du 12e chasseurs

Figure 59

187 The French Army of Reserve

Figure 60

Galy Montaglas was one of the few men who managed to escape the encirclement of the 12th Chasseurs. His memoires describe a running battle that was every bit as desperate as the one being fought at Marengo:

At Castellazzo the commander of the regiment placed two outposts on the banks of the Bormida, one commanded by Lt. Loquette and the other by Lt. Besson and we camped inside the village with half the regiment in the courtyard of a sort of chateau and the other in the courtyard of a farm and on the village square...None of us had slept the previous night and we were resting when suddenly someone called out, "Get to the horses!". We barely had time to reach the horses which were being kept in a field behind the village. At that same moment, a column of enemy hussars galloped into the village while another column attempted to encircle us to the rear of the village; this force was about 1,500 men strong, whilst we could barely muster 200 hussars. We attempted to resist but in vain; we were forced to flee at full gallop in trying to cross to the other side of the river bank before the enemy. We had lost over one hundred men as prisoners and many of us were wounded. We had hardly crossed and reformed on the other bank of the river, when the enemy were upon us again and with less than half our men we were forced to flee once more...We finally reached our own lines after over 6 hours of flight at full gallop... the regiment was reduced to just 93 officers and men, many of us wounded.
Montaglas

The role of the Chasseurs was to be a versatile, all-purpose light cavalry, able to take on every type of difficult or mundane task. Their roles included scouting, reconnaissance, supporting infantry and acting as a forward screen of pickets or skirmishers for the main army. Unlike the Hussars, their uniform was meant to be more standardised and practical. In practice, many Chasseur regiments were often brigaded with Hussars and developed a very similar culture and outlook. Antoine Nogues, the overworked aide to General Lannes records the type of missions undertaken by the 21st Chasseurs during the Marengo campaign:

'Lannes ordered me to reconnoitre the way ahead with a platoon of 25 chasseurs a cheval, while a squadron from the same regiment advanced along the main road. However, when our main squadron pulled back, some enemy Latour Dragoons attacked us from the woods close by. My horse was already lame from a bullet wound so I was soon overtaken and thought I would be captured or wounded. On the point of capture, I shot the closest of my pursuers with my pistol and just managed to reach safety and rejoin my General. The following day, we marched through Verchetti, Trino and Chivasco on the road to Pavia. At Trino, Lannes again ordered me to push on through the night with a platoon of

chasseurs on a reconnaissance towards the Po bridge. As we rode along the roadway, tired and exhausted, we suddenly found ourselves face to face with an enemy patrol, coming in the opposite direction. We had no sooner seen them, then we were charging after them. By now it was beginning to dawn and as we rode closer to the river, we could see a force of 200-300 enemy horsemen; at this point, I judged my mission accomplished and returned to give my report. I was then given yet another reconnaissance mission, though this time we encountered no-one and found the shore-line empty, so the army continued its advance towards Pavia.'
Memoires du General Nogues

Chasseurs were meant to use reconnaissance as a way of finding information about the enemy and searching for opportunities that might be exploited. Aubry of the 12th Chasseurs says that the period after Marengo saw a visible decline in the Austrian army, which his chasseurs experienced directly. He cites one example from the 1805 campaign:

'On this subject, I will mention a striking example. When the campaign opened against the Austrians, we thought this would be a serious matter. Marshal Davout had his division formed in battle-order and had deployed his forces; it was the beginning of the first cold weather spells, and we were feeling the effects. As night approached, the attack was postponed until the following day. A detachment of the 12th Chasseurs was ordered on a night reconnaissance. Our platoon of twenty-five men, wrapped in coats and cloaks, crossed the fields at a brisk pace, quickly reaching the point designated in our orders; we then returned without encountering the enemy. Yet on the following day, to our surprise, we found the fields we had travelled through littered with arms and equipment, but no enemy troops. The previous night, the enemy had been in camp and on hearing us approach had simply fled the field.'
Souvenirs de Captaine Aubry du 12e

Even in the late 1790s there were two versions of the Chasseur uniform. Figure 60 shows the more common form. It is based on a painting of a 12th Chasseur trooper from the Zurich manuscript dated 1799-1800. This first style of uniform was based on a dolman-style jacket, sometimes referred to as a 'caracot'. It was green for all regiments, with regimental colours on either cuffs, collar or both, and always piped white; it had 14-16 rows of white braid linked to 3 columns of pewter metal buttons. In this period, Chasseurs also wore braided waistcoats under their caracot, usually red but sometimes green.

The 12th Chasseurs had their regimental colour (red) on their collar and possibly their cuffs. Breeches were also always green, though on campaign, leather reinforced riding-trousers were also worn (usually over the breeches). The pattern on the breeches was always chevrons, with multiple chevrons denoting higher rank. Chasseurs also had the same thick green hooded cloak used by the Hussars. Boots were standard short light-cavalry boots.

The trooper in Figure 60 wears a new issue shako with a red and black flamme wound round it. A flexible leather peak has been tied to the front of the shako. The horse furniture is based on paintings by Hoffman and those in the Zurich manuscript; this includes the light infantry harness, the cylindrical valise and the sheepskin trimmed in the regimental colour. Elements of this style of Chasseur uniform can also be found in depictions by Devilly, Kobell and Labrousse as well as in other unsigned sources. Chasseurs appear to have braided their hair into cadenettes, in the style of the hussars.

The inset images show earlier forms of head-dress worn prior to 1800, including the Tarleton-like leather casquet and the ubiquitous mirliton and flamme.

The Chasseur of the 21st in Figure 59 is based on prints by Seele and prints in the Augsberger manuscript, which show uniforms based on the Habit-Long cavalry coat. Although this was an undress uniform for the Guard Chasseurs, ordinary regiments wore either the caracot-dolman or, occasionally, the Habit-Long coat. In 1800, very few regiments could boast of an 'undress uniform'; this luxury was the preserve of the guard or high-ranking officers. Seele's prints show figures wearing Habit coats with lapels and green turn-backs, including hunting horn symbols and piping in the regimental colour. Waistcoats could be of all varieties from red to striped yellow and green. Side-buttoned riding trousers had a strap which passed under the heel of the riding boots. Both these sources show headgear swathed in overlapping bands of 'flamme' material – usually black with coloured trim. The wrapped material was often so thick, it is often difficult to determine whether the headgear underneath is a simple felt mirliton or a new-style shako.

The Chasseur carries a version of the 1790-pattern Chasseur-a-cheval sabre; a practical all-purpose sword with a slightly curved 90 cm blade. It was massed produced throughout the 1790s in a number of workshop-factories including Dumont, Fleury and Caullier. He also carries a 1786-pattern cavalry carbine.

Chasseur Uniforms at Marengo

21st	Aurore collar only.
12th	Red collar and (in Zurich painting but not in regulations) red cuffs

Figure 61: Chef d'escadron Ismert: 11th Hussars: Supporting French infantry of 44th and 101st Line at La Stortigliona Farm and Cascina Bianca.

Figure 62: Colonel Fournier: 12th Hussars: Brigaded with the 21st Chasseurs and positioned north of Castel Ceriolo.

Apart from the 1st Hussars, the two Hussar regiments at Marengo were, like the Chasseurs, posted to the extreme flanks of the French positions.
The 200 men of the 11th Hussars had been posted to a position on the banks of the Bormida on the morning of the battle. Riding towards the sound of the guns, they took up positions at La Stortigliona farmhouse, which was being held and defended by companies from two battalions of the 44th and 101st Demi-Brigades. Arriving shortly before noon, the position was already being attacked by Croat Grenzer infantry. As the Austrian assault on Marengo grew more intense, troops from the 101st appear to have retreated, leaving their posts. This left the commanding officer, Aide-de-Camp Achille Dampierre, with about 500 infantry and one cannon to defend a now isolated farm complex far ahead of the French front line. By 2pm, Dampierre's unit had retreated to another more easily defended farm house, Cascina Bianca, some 500 metres further south. Here, surrounded and running short of ammunition, what remained of the 11th Hussars tried to break out and reach the main French force, leaving the infantry to their fate.

Report of Citizen Ismert, Chef d'escadron of the 11th regiment of hussars:
'On the 25th Prairial (14th June) General Victor sent us to the far left-flank to reconnoitre and to clear the area between the river and the Orba, of enemy troops. We scoured the area, becoming involved in a few minor skirmishes. At about half past eleven, as we recrossed the river, we came across a small battalion of the 44th Line defending an outpost (at La Stortigliona). An aide-de-camp of General Victor (Dampierre) came and ordered us to help defend this position. This we did, until about 2 o'clock, when the enemy, through force of numbers, forced us to retreat. By now we were without cannons or ammunition, whilst the enemy's artillery and infantry caused us many casualties. We retreated about 400 fathoms (800 metres). The enemy attacked us from all directions. Their cavalry, which had followed and surrounded us, executed a charge but the broken ground they had to cross caused some disorder in their ranks. I took advantage of this and made a counter-charge, breaking through

their lines and rallying my squadrons about 400-500 leagues (approx. 1 km) behind the enemy's line.
While the enemy were concentrating on fighting our remaining infantry (at Cascina Bianca) which I could no longer support, I gave orders to collect all fugitives. This search allowed us to collect about 50 infantrymen and 12 cavalrymen of the 2nd Cavalerie led by a captain; these men had been sent out on a foraging expedition before the battle. All these men were to prove very useful. I now divided my hussars into three sections; the right commanded by captain Sainte-Marie and the left wing commanded by captain Briche. The centre, together with the infantrymen and heavy cavalerie platoon, remained under my command. By now the enemy cavalry had caught up with us and were forming up in order to charge us. When the enemy charged, I had my infantry fire on them from concealed positions and then executed a counter-charge with my own hussars. The enemy became more careful now, continuing to pursue us but at a distance. The brave captain Briche noticed a column of enemy cavalry trying to outflank us on our left flank and drew them away from us, encouraging them to follow his hussars towards the river. This clever manoeuvre worked perfectly. So, by using every advantage offered by the terrain and by our formation, we managed to retreat towards San-Giuliano.
Ismert: published in Cugnac

Ismert had to abandon the fusiliers of the 44th Line under the command of Achille Dampierre. These 200-300 men had barricaded themselves within the farmhouse of Cascina Bianca, but without ammunition, they had no choice but to surrender.

Although not heavily committed in the fighting at Marengo, the 400 men of the 12th hussars had been in the fore-front of action throughout the campaign, having seen heavy fighting at the battle of Casteggio, just 5 days before Marengo. The 12th hussars (together with the 21st Chasseurs) had developed a reputation for indiscipline, refusing to obey orders during their passage through Switzerland and pillaging the town of Saint Pierre, amongst others. Towards the end of the battle, it was the 12th Hussars who attacked retreating Austrians from Second Column under Ott. According to General Watrin's report, they captured 3 cannons and one enemy flag.

'We now pursued the retreating enemy without allowing him respite. Three cannons and a number of caissons were captured by us as well as two flags, one captured by Citizen Lignere, hussar of the 12th regiment.'

Figure 61 is based on another highly detailed painting by Lejeune of a young senior officer of hussars in the early consulate, probably in campaign uniform. The colours of the 11th Hussars at Marengo are taken from two figures in

Lejeune's painting of Marengo and from two early depictions found in the Vinkhuijzen collection. The details are as they appear in Lejeune's painting. Despite the rather tattered appearance of the uniform, the four chevrons on breeches and sleeves mark this hussar as a senior officer; in this case a Chef d'escadron – a commander of 2 squadrons. It is interesting to note that the officer has a simple white lace dolman with about 10 rows of lace arranged along 5 columns of buttons. A raquette cord is fixed to his shako and a further raquette has been strung up behind the lace of his dolman. The fur on his pelisse is standard black. A black fabric 'flamme' with black silk trim has been wound around the shako. The rather battered peak of the shako appears to be fixed by two clips. His weapon is a 1786 hussar sabre with 85cm blade and a polished brass version of the scabbard. The details of the 11th hussar sabretache and saddle-cloth are taken from the above-mentioned sources. Also included, by way of comparison, is a sabretache of the 5th Hussars from the mid-1790s. The new sabretaches introduced under the consulate contrasted sharply with the style used during the earlier republic and directorate.

Figure 62 is based on a Hoffman painting of Colonel Fournier, the hapless commander of the unruly 12th Hussars; the note at the base of Hoffman's painting claimed it was based on a sketch made at Fort Bard at the start of the 1800 campaign. The uniform is the full dress uniform of a high-ranking officer, denoted by the 5 silver-thread chevrons on his breeches, sleeves and shako. The Colonel's dolman has possibly 14 rows of lace arranged in 5 columns of white metal buttons. The chevron design on the shako was not unusual for the period and Thevinin shows other light cavalry officers wearing similar shakos in his painting of the crossing of the St Bernard Pass. The officer's saddle cloth and sabretache are more ornate versions of the standard consular design. Belts for the 12th appear to have been black. The shako is fitted with a detachable peak, fixed by two buttons placed about an inch from the base of the shako. The highly ornate, metal studded bridle and horse furniture and leopard skin saddle cloth were all commonly used by hussar officers. Nogues had a very low opinion of Colonel Fournier, as his following account of the capture of Romano Bridge indicates:

The army, having arrived around Yvree, headed for the Romano bridge, which was defended by about 6,000 enemy troops. Attacked from the front and from both flanks, the enemy were pushed back from their positions. Meanwhile on the road, close to the bridge, an enemy cannon ball had destroyed the entire front line of the column, putting it into disorder. Lannes, seeing his men halting and losing their resolve, rode up to them saying "Soldiers! What! A cannonball's not going to stop you!"

194 The French Army of Reserve

Figure 61

195   The French Army of Reserve

Figure 62

Thereupon, he dismounted and sat down on the hole produced by the deadly ball saying, "I defy another one to come and hit us again!" His words gave the men courage once again, despite the fact that balls, shells and bullets continued to rain down upon us.
After the capture of the bridge, the 12th Hussars under the command of Colonel Fournier, received an order to charge and pursue the routed enemy. However, this Fournier was only brave at the distance of a pistol-shot, and although he may have brandished his sword in front of his regiment, he could neither organise his men nor lead them to victory.
Nogues

Fournier's pursuit along the road did not have the desired result and his men soon withdrew, allowing the Austrians to counter-attack once again. Within a few days, the 12th Hussars would be involved in a more successful action. This was to take place on the 9th June, 5 days before Marengo, at the more minor battle of Casteggio-Montebello. Nogues comments on the successful charge of the 12th which helped the French gain the initiative at the battle:

'The battle began all along the line. The noise of cannon fire and musketry was joined by the thunder and lightning of a storm which suddenly swept the battlefield with rain and hail; this momentarily disrupted the battle. Then, once again, fire and powder-smoke engulfed both armies as they advanced towards each other at bayonet point. At that moment, the 12th Hussars charged directly along the road, overthrowing the enemy, but were soon counterattacked and withdrew having sustained losses. However, our battalions had beaten the Austrian infantry which withdrew towards Voguera, covered by their strong and numerous cavalry.'
Nogues

Figure 63: Trooper: 1st 'Bercheny' Hussars: Attached to Desaix's division: Final French Counter-attack

Figure 64: Major: 1st 'Bercheny' Hussars: Attached to Desaix's division

The 150 men of 1st Hussars were from one single squadron, attached to Desaix's Corps.

They took part in a charge towards the very end of the battle, which was both significant and revealing. At this stage, towards 6pm, Austrian forward units had advanced along the road, beyond Cascina Grossa and had established pickets or outposts approaching San Giuliano. These pickets were almost certainly made up of light cavalry. The fact that Austrian patrols had advanced beyond Cascina Grossa shows the scale of the French retreat. The French army had retreated upwards of 5 kilometres in 4 hours and were still falling back.

The 1st Hussars rode in advance of Desaix's men, clearing the area. Kellerman states "The enemy skirmishers were repulsed until the village of Cascina Grossa".

"Captain de Juniac with the blue dolmans of Bercheny preceded Desaix's corps…it executed the boldest charge, killing 28 Austrians and making a number prisoner. Desaix took the name of Captain de Juniac who was in command to give to the first consul. He had successively removed 17 enemy posts; Hussar Bricogne-Visconti and Hussar Michel took the commanding officer of one post prisoner." Historique du 1e regiment de Hussards

The charge allowed Desaix's main infantry column to deploy north-east of Cascina Grossa . In particular, it was the 9th Legere that were able to deploy unobserved behind the tree-lined road leading to Cascina Grossa (today's Via della Liberta).

The trooper in Figure 63 is based on a painting by Kobell and another by Solomon Landolt, dated 1799.* The Hussar wears the colours of the 1st Bercheny regiment. He is in typical campaign dress, wearing side-buttoned riding trousers over his boots and breeches and the French version of the dolman (also called a caracot). As in the Kobell painting, this braided jacket was often worn open and unfastened over a braided waistcoat. Kobell shows it with a single shoulder strap on the left shoulder. A substantial length of 'flamme' material (black with red trim) has been wrapped around the head-gear so it is difficult to determine whether it is a mirliton or early shako. The flamme itself could be made from fabric or animal pelt. Hair is worn in cadenettes and a long queue. Much of his equipment is in undyed leather, including his cartridge pouch. He still has an old style of sabretache, issued in the time of the directorate. Although this style of campaign dress was rapidly falling out of favour, this represents what many 'other rank' hussars still looked like in 1800. The greater part of the 1st Hussars had been serving with the Army of Italy throughout 1799-1800. Marbot's memoires describe how although they had suffered severe shortages of everything, the 1st Hussars continued to put an emphasis on appearance:

'Although the uniforms of the revolutionary armies had become slovenly, the 1st Hussars continued to maintain their traditional uniform, as in the days when they

were the Bercheny Hussars. Moreover, where possible, all our hussars had to have a uniform appearance. This included wearing their hair in long queues and also braided cadenettes and turned-up moustaches. As I had none of these, my mentor Pertelay took me to the regimental barber where I bought tie-on queues and cadenettes. They fixed these to my own hair which was already long. Although I was embarrassed by this at first, I soon grew to like these hair extensions as they made me look like a veteran hussar. The moustaches presented a greater problem as I had no more facial hair than did a girl. Not wanting to spoil the uniformity of the regiment, Pertelay took a tin of black polish and with his thumb painted two enormous black hooks covering my upper lips and reaching almost to my eyes. This in turn caused a further problem. At the time our shakos had no peaks and so my face was exposed to the scorching rays of the Italian sun. On parades or on sentry duty, when I had to remain motionless, the heat would harden the black polish, contorting my skin very painfully. Yet I did not flinch. After all, I was a hussar.'
Marbot

Figure 64 is based on an early consulate painting of a 1st Hussar officer by Hoffman. If Figure 63 shows what Hussars looked like on campaign in Italy, then this image shows the full-dress uniforms adopted after Marengo and worn by officers on parade. The major difference was the adoption of the peaked shako, already used by Austrian Hussars. Indeed, shakos were already being issued in 1799-1800 and peaked versions were worn at least by officers and some light infantry and light cavalry, at the battle. However, contemporary depictions show shakos (or mirlitons) without peaks being far more common before 1801. This officer's shako is wrapped in a red and black silk flamme; the officer's consular sabretache is shown inset, as depicted by Hoffman.

Marbot relates one of the many minor battles fought by the 1st Hussars in the 1800 campaign:
*'The 1st Hussars attached to General Beaumont's brigade were placed on the extreme right of the French army. Our regiment had suffered casualties in preceding actions and could only put up three squadrons that day instead of the full four. There remained some thirty additional hussars, with 5 non-commissioned officers including myself and the brothers Pertelay…After an hour Pertelay perceived a battery of 8 guns in front of us, and consequently on the extreme left of the enemy's line; these guns were doing great damage to our ranks.
However, the enemy battery had been placed next to a small wood, from which it might be attacked. Pertelay planned to lead his small platoon there and attack the battery. His plan was to send us, one at a time, along a path that would take*

us to this small wood to the left of the battery. From there we could charge the guns from the flank and capture them, bringing them back to our army. The movement was carried out without being noticed by the enemy gunners. With young Pertelay leading us, we formed up, charged through the wood and reached the enemy battery, sabres in hand, just as they were firing their guns. We sabred some of the gunners but the others threw themselves under their ammunition caissons, where we could not attack them. Pertelay had given us orders not to sabre the artillery drivers but to force them to pull the guns as far as our own lines. We managed to do this for six of the guns, with the drivers remaining on their horses and following our orders. But the drivers of two of the guns had taken refuge under their horses and we were not able to make the horses move, however hard we pulled on their bridles. Meanwhile, the enemy infantry were running up to recapture their battery and time was running out. At last, Pertelay ordered us the leave the two remaining guns and to gallop back with the six we had been able to capture.'
Marbot

Being attached to one of the more well-known Hussar regiments was always considered a step above being a mere light cavalryman or Chasseur. Marbot did not take kindly to being transferred to the Chasseurs after the end of the Italian campaign:

'The minister sent me a commission in the 25th Chasseurs a cheval…I was deeply aggrieved by this transfer and felt that Bernadotte had misled me into believing I would get a place on Massena's staff or a commission in the 1st Hussars. Angry though I was, orders had to be obeyed…The chasseurs wore a green version of the hussar jacket, but I readily admit that giving up the uniform and name of the Bercheny Hussars for that of an ordinary chasseur caused me to shed a few tears. I set off in a foul temper.'
Marbot

*Kobell depicts a group of French hussars, painted in the period 1796-1800.

Hussar Uniforms at Marengo

The colours of hussar uniforms in 1800 were markedly different to the regulation colours adopted in the early empire. The colours below are based on contemporary sources including paintings by Hoffman.

1st	Sky-blue dolman and pelisse and breeches.
	Red collar and red cuffs with white braid.
	(sky blue collar after 1804)
12th	Brown dolman and pelisse and sky-blue breeches.
	Brown collar and sky-blue cuffs with white braid.
11th	Red dolman and green pelisse and sky-blue breeches.
	Red collar and red cuffs with white braid.

Figure 63

201   The French Army of Reserve

Figure 64

Figure 65: Fusilier: Polish Battalion: Attached to Italian Legion: Operating north of Milan

Figure 66: Horse Artillery: Italian Legion.
Figure 67: Fusilier: Italian Legion.
Figure 68: Lancer: Polish Light Cavalry Regiment: Attached to Italian Legion.

In considering the detailed events at Marengo, one might easily forget the wider context of the campaign and of the European conflict itself. Although the wars were essentially a territorial clash between rival European powers, the ideas of the French revolution, republicanism and nationhood had transformed the conflict into something markedly different. With good reason, many contemporary observers took the view that the principles of liberty, equality and fraternity could become excuses and fronts for French territorial expansion. Nevertheless, these ideas inspired strong popular sentiment and were to prove powerful forces in the new century. For example, French infantry at Marengo advanced on Austrian positions singing republican songs like the Marseillaise. The following is described by the French émigré, Louis Thevenet Danican;

It was half past 5 o'clock at Marengo and it was raining. We could hear the French singing and approaching from the east. We couldn't see them because of the rain but we could hear them. They were singing revolutionary songs and also military ribald songs about women, wine and food. A few bursts of cannon signalled the beginning of the attack. O'Reilly remained completely indifferent. He didn't even flinch when the French began their attack in earnest. Throughout this, they continued to sing and shout, "We want peace or death!" and "Advance, long live the Republic!"

Auguste Danican: Author of Les brigands demasques ou memoire pour server a l'histoire du temps present -quote taken from Marengo museum.

The Italian Legion is a case in point. The Legion had its roots in Italian republicanism. Napoleon had created a series of satellite republics in Italy following his successful Italian campaigns in 1796. These states also began a series of land and legal reforms which were to be as far reaching as those in France. When the Austrians attempted to regain control of their former territories in 1799, many republicans took refuge in France. Joining them were the Polish émigré troops who had garrisoned these territories. Bonaparte formed this disparate force into an Italian Legion, originally 4,300 men strong, with 2 battalions, 2 cavalry squadrons and a single light artillery battery. * Overall command was given to General Giuseppe Lecchi, with the Polish contingent commanded by Jean Henri Dombrowski. At the time of Marengo, the Legion was part of the Army of Reserve operating in the area of Lecco, north of Milan. It was tasked with guarding the approaches to this important city, still under French occupation.

It is possible that some units of Italian Legion artillery were at Marengo; an article at the Marengo museum suggests this and it is true that Napoleon tried to scrape together whatever artillery he could. However, the true significance of the Legion is the political leverage it gave the French. After Marengo, the Italian Legion became the nucleus of the army of the Cisalpine Republic. Flags and uniforms carried the slogan "Gli uomini liberi sono Fratelli" – all free men are brothers. Detachments from the Legion were sent to all occupied cities. As it marched through the city of Modena, the uniforms of its troops were painted and recorded by a priest, Antonio Rovatti; a man influenced by the ideas of the revolution. His intention was to "chronicle the memories of the principle events of my nation … with an impartial focus that respects all nations and with a commitment to offer to my readers a true vision and insight on the events I witnessed."

The early emblem of this revolutionary movement was not a flag but 'liberty trees' which were set up in every 'liberated' town square, often adorned with republican tricolore colours – red, blue and orange in Piedmont and red green and white elsewhere in Italy.

Figure 65 shows the uniform worn by Polish infantry fusiliers recorded by Rovatti. Rovatti's simple paintings may show the new uniforms adopted in 1800, when the Legion was resupplied at Nice. An earlier 1799 source by Rugendas, shows Polish troops wearing standard French infantry uniform. However, uniforms were fast becoming associated with national identity and Polish troops now wore the square sectioned Capzka, their national head-dress. Unlike French equipment, he also carries his short sword and bayonet on a waist-belt frog. His coat has light infantry lapels. Other details of the uniform are as shown. Rovatti also shows a Polish Grenadier who wears the same uniform, differentiated by red Capzka cords, a red plume, red epaulettes and a silver semi-circular metal plaque on the front of the Capzka (bearing an embossed grenade). The core of the Legion's Polish contingent were emigres, exiled after the partition of Poland, but most of the Poles were recruited from prisoners and deserters from the Austrian army.*** In turn, the Austrians treated captured Poles as deserters, not prisoners of war; many were court-martialled.

204 The French Army of Reserve

Figure 65

Figure 66

205   The French Army of Reserve

Figure 67

Figure 68

The Legion's Horse Artillery (Figure 66) also wore the Capzka, which suggests they may have been manned by Poles, most of whom had been granted citizenship by the republics. The uniform was based on a green cloth version of the fusilier's uniform, as shown. Rovatti also shows the uniform of Foot Artillery. This was similar to that of the Horse Artillery, except that they wore a bicorn with a rectangular Italian republican cockade (shown inset). The Artillery and Engineer College was based in Modena.

Appearing in the same section of his manuscript, Rovatti also recorded the uniform of Italian fusiliers of the 'Refugee Legion'. The uniform (Figure 67) was based on the French infantry coat, but in green cloth with red facings and white piping.** By now, red white and green were the republican tricolore colours adopted throughout most of northern Italy.

Figure 68 is based on an earlier 1799 tableau print of Polish Legion troops in Italy by Rugendas. The print shows cavalrymen wearing black Capzkas, though other figures in the tableau wear mirlitons (inset). In this print, troops are dressed in the style of French hussars; they wear long thigh-length caracote versions of the dolman, worn over a braided waistcoat, and side-buttoned riding trousers worn over breeches and light cavalry boots. An unusual feature is the zig-zag pattern of the red braid on the dolman, a style of braid sometimes used by Austrian hussars.

In 1799, on becoming Consul, Bonaparte had offered the leadership of a separate Polish Legion to the exiled General Tadeusz Kosciuszko. Kosciuszko refused, later commenting:

"The Emperor thinks only of himself, not about nationalist ideas and so he could not care less about any dreams of independence. He is a despot whose sole ambition is to satisfy his own personal ambition. He will create nothing of any permanence."

*According to French War Ministry Returns.
**Another source for the uniform of the Italian Legion is a print dated 1800 showing the rear aspect of a light infantryman with green uniform and yellow facings – despite there being very few details on the print, this has been taken as the basis for later depictions of Italian Legion troops. However, Rovatti is a more detailed, contemporary source and also an eyewitness. His manuscript is a detailed pictorial chronicle of uniforms covering the years 1796 to 1801.
***The émigré Hussar Francois de Cezac was posted to the part of Poland occupied by Russia and commented on the poverty and maltreatment of the rural population. At one point, he was billeted in a village where Cossacks arrived "with orders to kill all black dogs and to cut of the hair of all dark-haired women so they could collect material to make new shakos for a regiment of (Russian) hussars. This order caused panic in the village." Fortunately, he was able to save the daughter of his landlord by bribing the officer of the Cossacks.

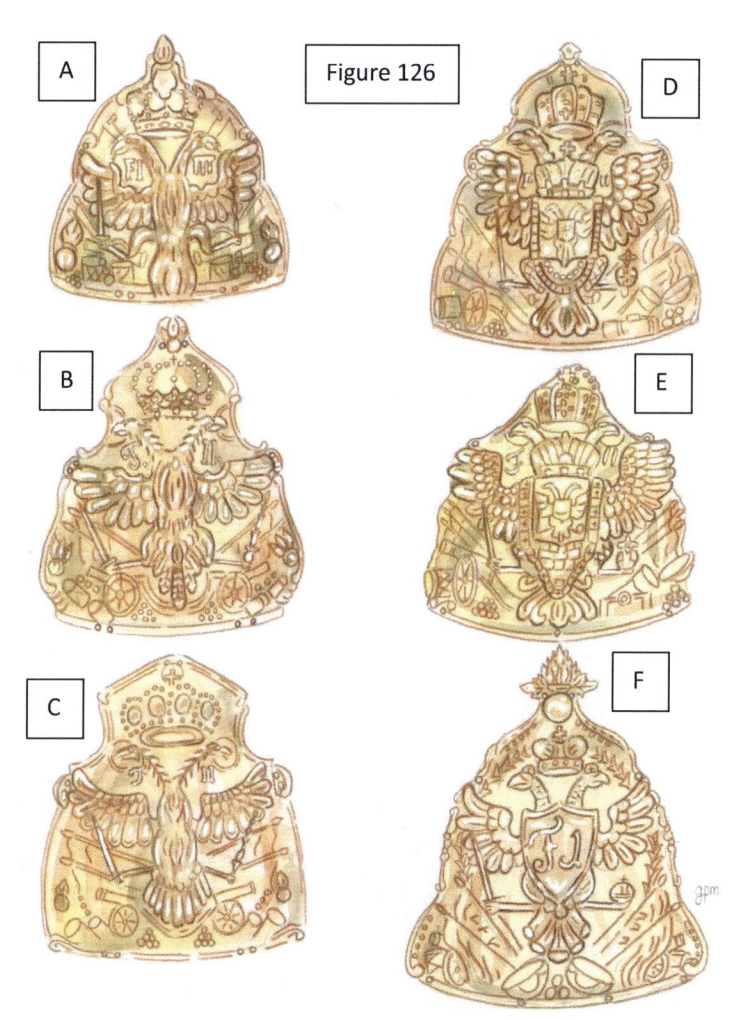

Figure 126: Austrian Grenadier Bearskin plates from 1760-1807
A: Plate from reign of Francis I and Maria Theresa. **B**. Plate from reign of Joseph II used until the 1790s. **C.** Plate from reign of Francis II in 1790s and early 1800s **D and E**. From 1804-05: Both plates show a double crown reflecting Francis II's reign as both Holy Roman Emperor and Austrian Emperor. Plate E is a gilt officer's plate produced in 1805; reflecting the hurried nature of mobilisation in 1805, it is of lower quality manufacture, being unsymmetrical, roughly cut and lacking a bordered edge. **F.** Plate produced after 1806, after Francis had adopted Francis I of Austria as his sole title. Mass produced, it lacks the studied symmetry of earlier designs.

Index of artists, printers, prints and collections

All of the painted figures in this book are based on a number of contemporary illustrated sources including paintings, prints and sketches; many of these are referenced in the text. This index provides an overview of the more important sources.
Paintings of military uniforms as with paintings of everyday life and people was not considered a fitting subject for high art in the 1800s. It was left to a category of artists who usually worked with engravers and publishers to produce commercial prints, mainly aquatints and lithographs. The black and white prints would then be coloured by colourists.

Almutter, Jacob Placidus 1780-1820: Austrian painter working in the Tyrol. As well as scenes of Tyrolean life, he painted soldiers and battlefields of the wars, often from life. His paintings and sketches of soldiers marching through the Tyrol, particularly French and Austrian troops, are highly detailed.

Appiani Andrea 1754-1818: Neoclassical artist and court painter to Napoleon's regime. His works include a series of portraits of Napoleon from the 1790s through to the Empire. Other portraits include Josephine and Eugene Beauharnais as well as General Louis Desaix.

ASKBL – Anne S K Brown Library: Anne Seddon Kinsolving Brown was an American heiress who amassed arguably the best military art archive in the world. Much of it is available online.

Artaria prints: Produced by the Artaria printing firm in Vienna, these are a series of prints of Austrian troops made throughout the 1790s bearing the title 'Scheme of all the uniforms of the Emperors'. The artist is named as Max Grimm. Located in the State Libraries of Darmstadt.

Auguste, Jean 1768-1825: French printer. Produced a tableau of French uniforms of the Grand Armee, printed in 1806.

Augsburg Prints: A series of prints produced between 1802 and 1809 in the city of Augsburg detailing uniforms from different countries – including works by artists Ebner, Rugendas, Seele and Voltz.

Barbier, Jean Francois 1754-1828: French soldier and painter. He is well known for his paintings of the 2nd Hussars between 1800 and 1805. Three of his paintings are of the Austerlitz campaign, in which he served and was wounded. Highly detailed watercolours based on his first-hand experiences.

Bleuler Johann Heinrich 1758-1823: Artist living in Zurich. Producer of paintings and prints showing both French and Austrian troops on the march in mid to late 1790s.

Brunswick Manuscript: see Muller C.

Bradford William: Produced a series of drawings mostly in private collections of uniforms of the armies of the consulate and other armies in the early 1800s and engraved by L. Clark and published in London by J. Booth, Portland Place, in 1809.

Index of Artists

Campe, Friederich 1777-1846: Nurembourg printer, produced prints of French army on campaign in 1806 campaign with detailed prints of French Horse Artillery. Worked in close association with the artist JM Voltz.

Detaille, Eduoard 1848-1912: Prominent late 19th century academic painter and military artist.

Duplessis-Bertaux, Jean: 1747-1818: French painter and engraver and professor of Drawing at the Ecole Militaire. Detailed drawings of French troops of the Consulate and early Empire.

Dryander Johann Friedrich 1756 – 1812: Painter of publicly and privately commissioned paintings of French Officers in the 1790s.

Ebner; Georg Christophe 1784-1863: Printer and publisher of works by German artists including Seele and Voltz.

Gautherot, Pierre Claude 1769-1825: French painter, commissioned to paint a formal painting for the 1805 campaign showing Napoleon addressing his troops at Augsberg. Includes detailed studies of French infantry uniforms.

Gerard, Francois Pascal 1770-1837: Prominent French painter commissioned by Napoleon to produce formal large-scale paintings of battle scenes including one of Austerlitz, each of which included highly detailed accurate studies of uniforms worn. Painted the portraits of the most prominent people of his time, including several of Napoleon.

Giesler (also Giessler); Christian Gottfried Heinrich 1770-1844: Painter and draughtsman and etcher. Worked in Russia during the 1790s and produced a series of detailed prints showing the French army in Germany in 1806.

Gros, Antoine Jean 1771-1835: Prominent painter commissioned by Napoleon to paint formal battle paintings including The Battle of Eylau as well as portraits of Napoleon himself.

Hauck, Auguste 1742-1801: Painter. Produced a series of acquatints of French republican soldiers in the mid-1700s recording their uniforms and equipment on campaign.

Hoffmann, Nicolaus 1740-1823: Artist and engraver. Produced a set of prints showing uniforms of the Royal French Army in the 1780s and of the French Republican Army of the revolution and consulate up to 1804-5. These are superbly detailed and can only have been produced from original sketches and drawings from life.

Kininger, Vicenz Georg 1767-1851: Austrian watercolour artist and draughtsman who worked closely with the printing firm of Tranquillo Mollo to produce superb studies of the new Austrian uniforms introduced after the 1798 army reforms. Also known for scenes from the early coalition wars depicting heroic actions of Austrian soldiers.

Knotel, Richard 1857-1914: Late 19th century German artist specialising in the study of uniforms. Worked on an encyclopaedia of uniforms, the Uniformenkunde.

Index of Artists

Kobell, Wilhelm von 1766-1853: One of the most important artists for early Napoleonic uniforms. A painter and printmaker based in Bavaria but who travelled widely throughout Europe. He produced a number of paintings of military reviews which allowed him to present very accurate detailed illustrations of the uniforms of major European armies, including those of Russia, Austria, France, Prussia and Bavaria. He also painted a number of earlier works showing French, Austrian and Russian troops on the march, with a similar eye to detail.

Langendijk Jan Anthonie 1780-1818: Dutch artist and engraver. Produced a series of detailed drawings showing the uniforms of French and Dutch soldiers between the period 1796-1805.

Langendyk Dirk 1748-1805: Dutch artist and etcher. Produced a series of superbly detailed drawings and prints showing soldiers of the 1790s on campaign, including French and Austrians. Details show the uniforms, equipment and also the variation in uniforms and how these were worn in the field. Most are based on original drawings from life.

Landolt, Salomon 1741-1818: Amateur artist and military painter based in Switzerland. Paintings, many of which are in the British Museum, show the true and quite appalling state and behaviour of armies on the march, including Russians, French and Austrians.

Lecomte, Hippolyte 1781-1857: French artist and brother-in-law of Vernet. Painted historical paintings but he also produced watercolour studies of soldiers from the early Empire including a Guard Hussar painted in 1807.

Lejeune; Baron Louis-Francois 1775-1848: French painter and active participant in the Napoleonic wars, Lejeune also left a vivid memoir of his experiences. Originally an aide to Napoleon, he later became a General. He was present at Marengo and Austerlitz and took part in the cavalry charge against the Russian Imperial Guard. A superb painter with highly detailed paintings of famous battles including Marengo and Austerlitz. His studies of people and uniforms are highly accurate and observed from real life. He also produced a series of watercolour studies of soldiers from the Consular period, some of which have survived in private collections. In 1806, he was instrumental in introducing new lithographic printing techniques to France.

Lethiere; Guillame Guillon 1760-1832: French painter and Professor at the Ecole des Beaux-Arts. Painter of a formally commissioned work depicting the Capture of the Tabor Bridge during the 1805 campaign.

Lussigny L (dates unknown): Artist known to have worked for the Beauharnais family with portraits of this family in private collections. Produced a highly detailed watercolour of a young Guard Chasseur dated 1799 in Italy owned by the ASKB. This is quite probably a painting of Eugene Beauharnais, painted for his mother, Josephine.

Martinet, Aaron 1762-1814: French printer and publisher who produced hundreds of uniform plates of the Grand Armee, of which 339 types survive. They span the years 1807 to 1814, though many of the plates are standard generic drawings recoloured differently to depict different regiments.

Index of Artists

Mollo, Tranquillo 1767-1837: Austrian printing publisher, including military prints. He is often associated with the engravers Adam Bartsch and Johann Georg Mansfeld and artist Vicenz Georg Kininger. He produced a key series of prints showing the new Austrian army uniforms introduced after 1798 as well as scenes from the early coalition wars in the 1790s to the early 1800s.

Muller, C (no known dates): Engraver and printer of Brunswick manuscript kept in Berlin State Library and in ASKB. The manuscript has 52 surviving prints of French uniforms from the Year 1805. Although the style is naive and some prints are evidently inaccurate or generic, certain prints are nevertheless important. They provide an eye-witness view of what how the French army appeared on campaign. Furthermore, even the more unusual details often correspond to similar details in other more reliable sources.

Ottenfeld, Rudolf von 1836-1914: Austrian late 19th century academic painter and military artist and a contemporary of Edouard Detaille. He provided the illustrations for Die österreichen Armee, 1770–1867 published in 1898 Vienna.

Otto manuscript: A set of 96 original bound watercolours of the Grand Armee and the Army of Italy dated to 1808 owned by the ASKB and of unknown origin and provenance. The ASKB suggest that the original artist may be CF Weiland or CW Kolbe. The manuscript nevertheless appears to be authentic and corresponds to other contemporary sources.

Pinhas, Soloman 1759-1813: German painter, best known for miniatures, based in Kassel where he became court painter. He also produced a series of paintings in 1810-11 of soldiers from the French-allied Kingdom of Westphalia.

'Poisson': Producer of a series of highly detailed prints and watercolours of uniforms of the Consular Guard, in private collections. The authors have copies of two surviving examples. Prints are marked: Paris chez Jean, Rue Jean de Beauvoir No3.

Potrelle, Jean Louis 1788-1824: French engraver and printer. Produced a set of 14 surviving prints of the French Consular Guard in 1801.

Rottmann Friedrich 1768-1816: Produced series of engravings in the early 1800s detailing events in the revolutionary wars between Austria and France.

Rovatti, Antonio 1763-1818: Italian priest with republican sympathies. Based in the city of Modena. Produced a chronicle with simple but detailed paintings of uniforms charting the wars fought in northern Italy between 1795 and 1805.

Rugendas, Johann Lorenz II 1775-1826: German artist born in to a family of engravers, artists and printers in Augsburg, known for their battle-scene prints. Produced a set of 35 prints of battle scenes spanning 15 years of the Napoleonic wars. Although not an eye-witness, the scenes include some very detailed, precise and accurate studies of the uniforms worn, often included as uniformed figures in the fore-ground. He could only have obtained these details by observing the uniforms first hand or by consulting original sketches.

Sauerweid, (also Zauerveid), Aleksander 1783-1844: Baltic painter and draughtsman born in Courland and working for various printers. He later became the Director of the St Petersburg Academy and painter to Czar Alexander's General Staff. Known for drawings of soldiers on campaign including Russian, French and Austrian soldiers before, during and after the 1805-06 campaigns. Unfortunately, many of his printed drawings have been dated to incorrectly '1813'; in fact they were drawn over a period spanning possibly over 15 years, from about 1800 to 1815. He painted a superb series of uniform studies of the Saxon army in 1810 and was commissioned by Alexander to paint a similar series of Russian uniforms in 1814.

Seele, Johann Baptiste 1774-1814: German artist and chronicler of the Coalition wars throughout the 1790s and early 1800s. Worked in co-operation with number of printing firms producing studies of soldiers from various armies. Showed the true nature of armies on the march, with studies of troops in bivouac and marauding, originally produced in watercolour. Also known for more formal portraiture, as with his portrait of the Archduke Charles. Possibly the main artist responsible for the Augsberg compendium of uniforms prints (see above).

Suhr, Christoph 1771-1842: German artist working for many years in Hamburg. A Professor at the Academy of Arts at Berlin, Christoph worked with his brothers, Cornelius (landscape painter) and Peter (printer and publisher) in a printing company in Hamburg. Most well known for producing a series of watercolours of French troops (mainly from 5th Corps) passing through Hamburg from 1806-1810; a collection known as the Bourgeois de Hambourg.

Thevinin Charles 1764-1838: Artist who produced a series of officially commissioned paintings for the revolutionary governments, directorate, consulate and empire. Later becoming director of the French Academy in Rome. His works include the Surrender at Ulm and the Crossing of the St Bernard Pass, both of which contain highly detailed studies of soldiers and uniforms.

Vaquirron (Vagrisson) – other details unknown: Artist named in Brunswick manuscript printed by C Muller in 1805 (see Muller).

Vernet, Carle (formerly Antoine Charles Horace) 1758-1836: Prominent French painter and lithographer and father of Horace Vernet. His career as an artist was disrupted by the revolution, when his sister was sent to the guillotine. He then gained prominence under Napoleon with battle-scenes such as the Morning of Austerlitz. His formal paintings are very much part of the deliberate mythologising of Napoleon undertaken by the Imperial regime in all spheres of art.

Vernet, Horace 1789-1863: Prominent French painter and son of Carle Vernet. He gained prominence under Louis Philip who commissioned him to paint a number of French battle paintings in the 1830s to be included in the Gallery of Historical Art at Versailles. Three of his best known works include those of Napoleon at the battles of Jena, Wagram and Friedland painted in 1836-8. Vernet's paintings always figure an idealised image of Napoleon as the central focus, surrounded by his troops in full uniform. However, the uniformed figures included in each of these paintings are highly accurate and Vernet was a contemporary to the events he painted.

Index of Artists

Vinkhuijzen, Henrik Jacobus 1843-1910: Dutch collector of prints and watercolours. His collection of 32,000 prints is curated by the New York Public Library. Although most prints are from later 19th century books and magazines, a few are contemporary or near contemporary illustrations. Others also provide important details on uniform, corroborated by more reliable earlier sources. A superb archive.

Voltz, Johann Michael 1784-1858: German caricaturist and artist working for printing publishers. Possibly one of the contributors to the Augsberg prints. Known for two prints in 1805 showing Austrian prisoners from Ulm and Russian prisoners from Austerlitz.

Weber, Franz Thomas 1761-1828: German artist and engraver working in Augsberg. Produced a series of prints of the Russian army of 1799 under Czar Paul.

Weiland,C.F: (see Otto manuscript) Wurttemberg Army Officer and commercial artist.

Zimmermann Charles: Artist of 62 ink drawings of the Grand Armee dated as 1808. However, the date 1808 has been added to each drawing in different coloured ink and it is probable that many of the drawings were drawn earlier than 1808 and relate to uniforms in the 1806-07 campaign in Germany.

Zurich Manuscript: Produced by an unknown artist. Kept in the Zentralbibliothek Zürich and printed by Leonhard Zielgler. It shows a series of simple but very detailed drawings of French, Austrian and Swiss soldiers from the period 1799-1800, many of these troops being part of the Army of Reserve.

Zix Benjamin 1772-1811: Artist and producer of etchings and engravings detailing soldiers on the march or in camp. Highly detailed and probably based on sketches in the field.

Selected Bibliography

Arnold James R: Marengo and Hohenlinden, Pen and Sword 2005

Aubry Thomas Joseph: Souvenirs de 12e Chasseurs 1799-1815 Publisher Maison Quantin 1889

Barrès, Jean-Baptiste-AugusteTitle : Souvenirs d'un officier de la Grande Armée (11e éd.) / [Jean Baptiste Auguste Barrès] ; publiés par Maurice Barrès, son petit-filsnnnnAuthor : Barrès, Jean-Baptiste-Auguste (1784-1848). Auteur du texte Publisher : (Paris)Publication date : 1923

Beauharnais, Eugene – see Eugene

Bigarre – Memoires du general Bigarre 1775-1813 Paris; Grenadier 2002

Blaze, Elzéar Title : La Vie militaire sous le Premier Empire, ou Moeurs de garnison, du bivouac ou de la caserne, par E. Blaze,...Author : Blaze, Elzéar (1788-1848). Auteur du texte Publisher : (Paris) Publication date : 1888

Brinner, Wilhelm - Geschichte des k.k. Pionnier-Regimentes, Publication Vienna 1878

Brizzi GP Modena napoleonica nella Cronaca di Antonio Rovatti. 1796-1797 Fondazione Cassa di Risparmio di Modena, 1995

Bukhari Emir, French Napoleonic Line Infantry Almark 1973

Bukhari Emir, Naploeon's Cavalry Osprey 1979

Cézac, François de - Souvenirs de François de Cézac, hussard de Berchény, volontaire à l'armée de Condé : dix ans d'émigration (1791-1801) / publiés par le Baron A. de Maricourt, Publisher : Émile- Paul (Paris) 1909

Chandler, David, The Campaigns of Napoleon, London 1967.

Coignet, Jean-Roch Title : Souvenirs d'un vieux grognard , par le capitaine J.-R. Coignet Author : Coignet, Jean-Roch (1776-1865). Auteur du texte Publisher : J. Tallandier (Paris)Publication date : 1912

Comeau de Charry, Sébastien Joseph deTitle : Souvenirs des guerres d'Allemagne pendant la Révolution et l'Empire / par le Baron de Comeau,... Author : Comeau de Charry, Sébastien Joseph de (1771-1844). Auteur du texte Publisher : (Paris) Publication date : 1900

Crossard Jean Baptiste L. baron de - Mémoires militaires et historiques pour servir à l'histoire de la guerre Volume 2, Paris 1829

Crowdy TE : Marengo – Pen and Sword 2018 -Recommended Text

Cugnac, Gaspar Jean Marie René de - Campagne de l'armée de réserve en 1800. Publ. État-major de l'armée. Section historique R. Chapelot et ce., 1900

Danican Auguste: Les brigands demasques ou memoire pour server a l'histoire du temps present 1797
Dempsey Guy C Napoleon's Army 1807-1815 The Martinet Prints Arms and Armour Press 1997
Dempsey Guy C Napoleon's Soldiers – The Otto Manuscript Arms and Armour Press 1994
Duffy, Christopher, Austerlitz 1805, London 1977.

Bibliography

Eugène de Beauharnais Prince, Mémoires et correspondance politique et militaire du prince Eugène, , Albert Du Casse Published by Levy Brothers 1858

Gachot Edouard - La deuxième Campagne d'Italie en 1800, Paris 1899

Glover M, The Napoleonic Wars Anchor Press 1980

Gonneville, Aymar-Olivier Le Harivel de Recollections of Colonel de Gonneville by Gonneville, Aymar-Olivier Le Harivel de, 1783-1872; Mirabeau, Marie de Gonneville, comtesse de, 1829- [from old catalog]; Ambert, Joachim-Marie-Jean-Jacques-Alexandre-Jules, 1804-1890; Publication date 1875 Publisher London, Hurst and Blackett

Haythornthwaite Philip   The Austrian Army of the Napoleonic Wars - Cavalry Osprey 1986
Haythornthwaite Philip   The Austrian Army of the Napoleonic Wars - Infantry Osprey 1986

Hollins David: Marengo 1800, Osprey 2000

Hüffer, Hermann - Quellen zur geschichte der kriege von 1799 und 1800, aus den sammlungen des K. und k. kriegsarchivs, des haus, hof, -und staatsarchivs und des archivs des erzherzogs Albrecht in Wien by Leipzig, B.G. Teubner, 1900

Kellermann, François-Étienne - Réfutation de M. le duc de Rovigo, ou La vérité sur la bataille de Marengo Publisher : Rosier (Paris)   1828

Krettly, Élie - Souvenirs historiques du capitaine Krettly, ancien trompette major des guides d'Italie; Publisher : Biard 1838

Lejeune, Louis François, Baron Memoirs of Baron Lejeune, aide-de-camp to marshals Berthier, Davout, and Oudinot; by Lejeune, Louis François, Baron, 1775-1848; D'Anvers, N., d. 1933, ed. and tr; Maurice, John Frederick, Sir, 1841-1912 Publication date 1897
Publisher: Green, and Co.

Levavasseur, Octave Title : Un officier d'état-major sous le premier Empire : souvenirs militaires d'Octave Levavasseur, officier d'artillerie, aide-de-camp du maréchal Ney (1802-1815) / publiés par le commandant Beslay Author : Levavasseur, Octave (1781-1866).

Marbot, Marcellin de - Mémoires du général baron de Marbot. Gênes-Austerlitz-Eylau, Plon-Nourrit (Paris) 1891

Marmont, Auguste-Frédéric-Louis - Mémoires du maréchal Marmont, duc de Raguse, Paris 1857

Masson, Frédéric, Aventures de Guerre 1792–1809, Paris 1894 (reprinted 2003).

Montaglas, Jean-Pierre-Galy - Historique du 12e chasseurs à cheval, depuis le 29 avril 1792 jusqu'au traité de Lunéville (9 février 1801) : mémoires inédits du chef d'escadrons Galy Montaglas, du 12e chasseurs – Publisher : Chapelot 1908

Montholon, Charles Tristan - Napoléon Ier empereur des Français - Mémoires pour servir à l'histoire de France, sous Napoléon : écrits à Sainte-Hélène par les généraux qui ont partagé sa captivité, et publiés sur les manuscrits entièrement corrigés de la main de Napoléon. écrit par le général comte de Montholon Firmin Didot-père et fils (Paris) 1825

Napoléon Ier empereur des Français - Mémoires de Napoléon Bonaparte . Manuscrit venu de Sainte-Hélène, Paris 1821

Neipperg Adam Adalbert : Apercu militaire sur la bataille de Marengo published in Huffer (see above).

Noguès, Antoine - Mémoires du général Noguès, sur les guerres de l'Empire / publiés par le baron André de Maricourt, Publisher : A. Lemerre 1922

Ogier d'Ivry, Édouard Louis Marie
Historique du 9e régiment de hussards et des guides de la garde,par le commandant Ogier d'Ivry
Historique du 1er régiment de hussards: Valence 1891

Ottenfeld von R – Die Oesterreichische Armee, Vienna 1895

Petit, Joseph - Marengo: Or The Campaign of Italy, by the Army of Reserve. Transl by C Foudras, Publ. Philadelphia USA 1801

Petit, Joseph – Maringo ou la campagne d'Italie par l'armee de reserve, Paris 1800

Rapp, Jean Title : Mémoires du général Rapp, aide-de-camp de Napoléon , écrits par lui-même et publiés par sa famille Author : Rapp, Jean (1773-1821). Auteur du texte Publisher : (Paris) Publication date : 1823

Radetzky Josef Wenzel Graf - Erinnerungen an das Leben und die Thaten des k. k. Feldmarschalls Josef Wenzel Graf Radetzky von Radetz, Mayer, 1858

Rauch, Josef - Erinnerungen eines Offiziers aus Altösterreich, Munich,1918

Rothenberg Gunther E – Napoleon's Great Adversaries; Archduke Charles and the Austrian Army. Da Cap Press 1982

Rousselot Lucien L'armee Francais

Rovatti, Antonio: La Cronaca Rovatti – edited by Giancarlo Boeri – La Rivista Militare 1989

Savary, Anne-Jean-Marie-René - Mémoires du duc de Rovigo, pour servir à l'histoire de l'empereur Napoléon. Paris 1828

Segur, Philip Paul Comte de - Histoire et Memoires Vol 2 Firmin Didot Brothers Publ 1873

Stutterhiem Joseph: Die schlacht von Marengo (published in Huffer)
Stutterheim Karl von: La Bataille d'Austerlitz par un militaire – Karl von Stutterheim 1806 Hambourg

Thiébault, Paul Title : Mémoires du général Bon Thiébault. T. 1 Author : Thiébault, Paul (1769-1846). Publisher : (Paris) Publication date : 1893-1895
Truenfest, Amon von Truenfest Geschichte des k. k. 11. Husaren regimentes Herzog Vienna 1878

Victor, Claude-Victor Perrin, duc de Bellune - Extraits des Mémoires inédits - Campagne de l'armée de réserve en l'an VIII, Publisher : J. Dumaine (Paris) 1848